C-3274 CAREER EXAMINATION SERIES

This is your
PASSBOOK for...

Clerk IV

Test Preparation Study Guide
Questions & Answers

NLC®

NATIONAL LEARNING CORPORATION®

National Learning Corporation

212 Michael Drive, Syosset, NY 11791
(516) 921-8888 • www.passbooks.com
E-mail: info@passbooks.com

PUBLISHED IN THE UNITED STATES OF AMERICA

PASSBOOK® SERIES

THE *PASSBOOK® SERIES* has been created to prepare applicants and candidates for the ultimate academic battlefield – the examination room.

At some time in our lives, each and every one of us may be required to take an examination – for validation, matriculation, admission, qualification, registration, certification, or licensure.

Based on the assumption that every applicant or candidate has met the basic formal educational standards, has taken the required number of courses, and read the necessary texts, the *PASSBOOK® SERIES* furnishes the one special preparation which may assure passing with confidence, instead of failing with insecurity. Examination questions – together with answers – are furnished as the basic vehicle for study so that the mysteries of the examination and its compounding difficulties may be eliminated or diminished by a sure method.

This book is meant to help you pass your examination provided that you qualify and are serious in your objective.

The entire field is reviewed through the huge store of content information which is succinctly presented through a provocative and challenging approach – the question-and-answer method.

A climate of success is established by furnishing the correct answers at the end of each test.

You soon learn to recognize types of questions, forms of questions, and patterns of questioning. You may even begin to anticipate expected outcomes.

You perceive that many questions are repeated or adapted so that you can gain acute insights, which may enable you to score many sure points.

You learn how to confront new questions, or types of questions, and to attack them confidently and work out the correct answers.

You note objectives and emphases, and recognize pitfalls and dangers, so that you may make positive educational adjustments.

Moreover, you are kept fully informed in relation to new concepts, methods, practices, and directions in the field.

You discover that you are actually taking the examination all the time: you are preparing for the examination by "taking" an examination, not by reading extraneous and/or supererogatory textbooks.

In short, this PASSBOOK®, used directedly, should be an important factor in helping you to pass your test.

CLERK IV

DUTIES
Performs, plans, assigns and supervises a variety of difficult and specialized clerical work. Performs related duties as required.

SUBJECT OF EXAMINATION
The written test will be designed to test for knowledge, skills, and/or abilities in such areas as:

1. Office record keeping;
2. Preparing written material;
3. Supervision;
4. Understanding and interpreting written material; and
5. Office management.

HOW TO TAKE A TEST

I. YOU MUST PASS AN EXAMINATION

A. WHAT EVERY CANDIDATE SHOULD KNOW

Examination applicants often ask us for help in preparing for the written test. What can I study in advance? What kinds of questions will be asked? How will the test be given? How will the papers be graded?

As an applicant for a civil service examination, you may be wondering about some of these things. Our purpose here is to suggest effective methods of advance study and to describe civil service examinations.

Your chances for success on this examination can be increased if you know how to prepare. Those "pre-examination jitters" can be reduced if you know what to expect. You can even experience an adventure in good citizenship if you know why civil service exams are given.

B. WHY ARE CIVIL SERVICE EXAMINATIONS GIVEN?

Civil service examinations are important to you in two ways. As a citizen, you want public jobs filled by employees who know how to do their work. As a job seeker, you want a fair chance to compete for that job on an equal footing with other candidates. The best-known means of accomplishing this two-fold goal is the competitive examination.

Exams are widely publicized throughout the nation. They may be administered for jobs in federal, state, city, municipal, town or village governments or agencies.

Any citizen may apply, with some limitations, such as the age or residence of applicants. Your experience and education may be reviewed to see whether you meet the requirements for the particular examination. When these requirements exist, they are reasonable and applied consistently to all applicants. Thus, a competitive examination may cause you some uneasiness now, but it is your privilege and safeguard.

C. HOW ARE CIVIL SERVICE EXAMS DEVELOPED?

Examinations are carefully written by trained technicians who are specialists in the field known as "psychological measurement," in consultation with recognized authorities in the field of work that the test will cover. These experts recommend the subject matter areas or skills to be tested; only those knowledges or skills important to your success on the job are included. The most reliable books and source materials available are used as references. Together, the experts and technicians judge the difficulty level of the questions.

Test technicians know how to phrase questions so that the problem is clearly stated. Their ethics do not permit "trick" or "catch" questions. Questions may have been tried out on sample groups, or subjected to statistical analysis, to determine their usefulness.

Written tests are often used in combination with performance tests, ratings of training and experience, and oral interviews. All of these measures combine to form the best-known means of finding the right person for the right job.

II. HOW TO PASS THE WRITTEN TEST

A. NATURE OF THE EXAMINATION

To prepare intelligently for civil service examinations, you should know how they differ from school examinations you have taken. In school you were assigned certain definite pages to read or subjects to cover. The examination questions were quite detailed and usually emphasized memory. Civil service exams, on the other hand, try to discover your present ability to perform the duties of a position, plus your potentiality to learn these duties. In other words, a civil service exam attempts to predict how successful you will be. Questions cover such a broad area that they cannot be as minute and detailed as school exam questions.

In the public service similar kinds of work, or positions, are grouped together in one "class." This process is known as *position-classification*. All the positions in a class are paid according to the salary range for that class. One class title covers all of these positions, and they are all tested by the same examination.

B. FOUR BASIC STEPS

1) Study the announcement

How, then, can you know what subjects to study? Our best answer is: "Learn as much as possible about the class of positions for which you've applied." The exam will test the knowledge, skills and abilities needed to do the work.

Your most valuable source of information about the position you want is the official exam announcement. This announcement lists the training and experience qualifications. Check these standards and apply only if you come reasonably close to meeting them.

The brief description of the position in the examination announcement offers some clues to the subjects which will be tested. Think about the job itself. Review the duties in your mind. Can you perform them, or are there some in which you are rusty? Fill in the blank spots in your preparation.

Many jurisdictions preview the written test in the exam announcement by including a section called "Knowledge and Abilities Required," "Scope of the Examination," or some similar heading. Here you will find out specifically what fields will be tested.

2) Review your own background

Once you learn in general what the position is all about, and what you need to know to do the work, ask yourself which subjects you already know fairly well and which need improvement. You may wonder whether to concentrate on improving your strong areas or on building some background in your fields of weakness. When the announcement has specified "some knowledge" or "considerable knowledge," or has used adjectives like "beginning principles of..." or "advanced ... methods," you can get a clue as to the number and difficulty of questions to be asked in any given field. More questions, and hence broader coverage, would be included for those subjects which are more important in the work. Now weigh your strengths and weaknesses against the job requirements and prepare accordingly.

3) Determine the level of the position

Another way to tell how intensively you should prepare is to understand the level of the job for which you are applying. Is it the entering level? In other words, is this the position in which beginners in a field of work are hired? Or is it an intermediate or advanced level? Sometimes this is indicated by such words as "Junior" or "Senior" in the class title. Other jurisdictions use Roman numerals to designate the level – Clerk I, Clerk II, for example. The word "Supervisor" sometimes appears in the title. If the level is not indicated by the title, check the description of duties. Will you be working under very close supervision, or will you have responsibility for independent decisions in this work?

4) Choose appropriate study materials

Now that you know the subjects to be examined and the relative amount of each subject to be covered, you can choose suitable study materials. For beginning level jobs, or even advanced ones, if you have a pronounced weakness in some aspect of your training, read a modern, standard textbook in that field. Be sure it is up to date and has general coverage. Such books are normally available at your library, and the librarian will be glad to help you locate one. For entry-level positions, questions of appropriate difficulty are chosen – neither highly advanced questions, nor those too simple. Such questions require careful thought but not advanced training.

If the position for which you are applying is technical or advanced, you will read more advanced, specialized material. If you are already familiar with the basic principles of your field, elementary textbooks would waste your time. Concentrate on advanced textbooks and technical periodicals. Think through the concepts and review difficult problems in your field.

These are all general sources. You can get more ideas on your own initiative, following these leads. For example, training manuals and publications of the government agency which employs workers in your field can be useful, particularly for technical and professional positions. A letter or visit to the government department involved may result in more specific study suggestions, and certainly will provide you with a more definite idea of the exact nature of the position you are seeking.

III. KINDS OF TESTS

Tests are used for purposes other than measuring knowledge and ability to perform specified duties. For some positions, it is equally important to test ability to make adjustments to new situations or to profit from training. In others, basic mental abilities not dependent on information are essential. Questions which test these things may not appear as pertinent to the duties of the position as those which test for knowledge and information. Yet they are often highly important parts of a fair examination. For very general questions, it is almost impossible to help you direct your study efforts. What we can do is to point out some of the more common of these general abilities needed in public service positions and describe some typical questions.

1) General information

Broad, general information has been found useful for predicting job success in some kinds of work. This is tested in a variety of ways, from vocabulary lists to questions about current events. Basic background in some field of work, such as sociology or economics, may be sampled in a group of questions. Often these are principles which have become familiar to most persons through exposure rather than through formal training. It is difficult to advise you how to study for these questions; being alert to the world around you is our best suggestion.

2) Verbal ability

An example of an ability needed in many positions is verbal or language ability. Verbal ability is, in brief, the ability to use and understand words. Vocabulary and grammar tests are typical measures of this ability. Reading comprehension or paragraph interpretation questions are common in many kinds of civil service tests. You are given a paragraph of written material and asked to find its central meaning.

3) Numerical ability

Number skills can be tested by the familiar arithmetic problem, by checking paired lists of numbers to see which are alike and which are different, or by interpreting charts and graphs. In the latter test, a graph may be printed in the test booklet which you are asked to use as the basis for answering questions.

4) Observation

A popular test for law-enforcement positions is the observation test. A picture is shown to you for several minutes, then taken away. Questions about the picture test your ability to observe both details and larger elements.

5) Following directions

In many positions in the public service, the employee must be able to carry out written instructions dependably and accurately. You may be given a chart with several columns, each column listing a variety of information. The questions require you to carry out directions involving the information given in the chart.

6) Skills and aptitudes

Performance tests effectively measure some manual skills and aptitudes. When the skill is one in which you are trained, such as typing or shorthand, you can practice. These tests are often very much like those given in business school or high school courses. For many of the other skills and aptitudes, however, no short-time preparation can be made. Skills and abilities natural to you or that you have developed throughout your lifetime are being tested.

Many of the general questions just described provide all the data needed to answer the questions and ask you to use your reasoning ability to find the answers. Your best preparation for these tests, as well as for tests of facts and ideas, is to be at your physical and mental best. You, no doubt, have your own methods of getting into an exam-taking mood and keeping "in shape." The next section lists some ideas on this subject.

IV. KINDS OF QUESTIONS

Only rarely is the "essay" question, which you answer in narrative form, used in civil service tests. Civil service tests are usually of the short-answer type. Full instructions for answering these questions will be given to you at the examination. But in case this is your first experience with short-answer questions and separate answer sheets, here is what you need to know:

1) Multiple-choice Questions

Most popular of the short-answer questions is the "multiple choice" or "best answer" question. It can be used, for example, to test for factual knowledge, ability to solve problems or judgment in meeting situations found at work.

A multiple-choice question is normally one of three types—

- It can begin with an incomplete statement followed by several possible endings. You are to find the one ending which *best* completes the statement, although some of the others may not be entirely wrong.
- It can also be a complete statement in the form of a question which is answered by choosing one of the statements listed.

- It can be in the form of a problem – again you select the best answer.

Here is an example of a multiple-choice question with a discussion which should give you some clues as to the method for choosing the right answer:

When an employee has a complaint about his assignment, the action which will *best* help him overcome his difficulty is to

A. discuss his difficulty with his coworkers
B. take the problem to the head of the organization
C. take the problem to the person who gave him the assignment
D. say nothing to anyone about his complaint

In answering this question, you should study each of the choices to find which is best. Consider choice "A" – Certainly an employee may discuss his complaint with fellow employees, but no change or improvement can result, and the complaint remains unresolved. Choice "B" is a poor choice since the head of the organization probably does not know what assignment you have been given, and taking your problem to him is known as "going over the head" of the supervisor. The supervisor, or person who made the assignment, is the person who can clarify it or correct any injustice. Choice "C" is, therefore, correct. To say nothing, as in choice "D," is unwise. Supervisors have and interest in knowing the problems employees are facing, and the employee is seeking a solution to his problem.

2) True/False Questions

The "true/false" or "right/wrong" form of question is sometimes used. Here a complete statement is given. Your job is to decide whether the statement is right or wrong.

SAMPLE: A roaming cell-phone call to a nearby city costs less than a non-roaming call to a distant city.

This statement is wrong, or false, since roaming calls are more expensive.

This is not a complete list of all possible question forms, although most of the others are variations of these common types. You will always get complete directions for answering questions. Be sure you understand *how* to mark your answers – ask questions until you do.

V. RECORDING YOUR ANSWERS

Computer terminals are used more and more today for many different kinds of exams.

For an examination with very few applicants, you may be told to record your answers in the test booklet itself. Separate answer sheets are much more common. If this separate answer sheet is to be scored by machine – and this is often the case – it is highly important that you mark your answers correctly in order to get credit.

An electronic scoring machine is often used in civil service offices because of the speed with which papers can be scored. Machine-scored answer sheets must be marked with a pencil, which will be given to you. This pencil has a high graphite content which responds to the electronic scoring machine. As a matter of fact, stray dots may register as answers, so do not let your pencil rest on the answer sheet while you are pondering the correct answer. Also, if your pencil lead breaks or is otherwise defective, ask for another.

Since the answer sheet will be dropped in a slot in the scoring machine, be careful not to bend the corners or get the paper crumpled.

The answer sheet normally has five vertical columns of numbers, with 30 numbers to a column. These numbers correspond to the question numbers in your test booklet. After each number, going across the page are four or five pairs of dotted lines. These short dotted lines have small letters or numbers above them. The first two pairs may also have a "T" or "F" above the letters. This indicates that the first two pairs only are to be used if the questions are of the true-false type. If the questions are multiple choice, disregard the "T" and "F" and pay attention only to the small letters or numbers.

Answer your questions in the manner of the sample that follows:

32. The largest city in the United States is
    A. Washington, D.C.
    B. New York City
    C. Chicago
    D. Detroit
    E. San Francisco

1) Choose the answer you think is best. (New York City is the largest, so "B" is correct.)
2) Find the row of dotted lines numbered the same as the question you are answering. (Find row number 32)
3) Find the pair of dotted lines corresponding to the answer. (Find the pair of lines under the mark "B.")
4) Make a solid black mark between the dotted lines.

VI. BEFORE THE TEST

Common sense will help you find procedures to follow to get ready for an examination. Too many of us, however, overlook these sensible measures. Indeed, nervousness and fatigue have been found to be the most serious reasons why applicants fail to do their best on civil service tests. Here is a list of reminders:

- Begin your preparation early – Don't wait until the last minute to go scurrying around for books and materials or to find out what the position is all about.
- Prepare continuously – An hour a night for a week is better than an all-night cram session. This has been definitely established. What is more, a night a week for a month will return better dividends than crowding your study into a shorter period of time.
- Locate the place of the exam – You have been sent a notice telling you when and where to report for the examination. If the location is in a different town or otherwise unfamiliar to you, it would be well to inquire the best route and learn something about the building.
- Relax the night before the test – Allow your mind to rest. Do not study at all that night. Plan some mild recreation or diversion; then go to bed early and get a good night's sleep.
- Get up early enough to make a leisurely trip to the place for the test – This way unforeseen events, traffic snarls, unfamiliar buildings, etc. will not upset you.
- Dress comfortably – A written test is not a fashion show. You will be known by number and not by name, so wear something comfortable.

- Leave excess paraphernalia at home – Shopping bags and odd bundles will get in your way. You need bring only the items mentioned in the official notice you received; usually everything you need is provided. Do not bring reference books to the exam. They will only confuse those last minutes and be taken away from you when in the test room.
- Arrive somewhat ahead of time – If because of transportation schedules you must get there very early, bring a newspaper or magazine to take your mind off yourself while waiting.
- Locate the examination room – When you have found the proper room, you will be directed to the seat or part of the room where you will sit. Sometimes you are given a sheet of instructions to read while you are waiting. Do not fill out any forms until you are told to do so; just read them and be prepared.
- Relax and prepare to listen to the instructions
- If you have any physical problem that may keep you from doing your best, be sure to tell the test administrator. If you are sick or in poor health, you really cannot do your best on the exam. You can come back and take the test some other time.

VII. AT THE TEST

The day of the test is here and you have the test booklet in your hand. The temptation to get going is very strong. Caution! There is more to success than knowing the right answers. You must know how to identify your papers and understand variations in the type of short-answer question used in this particular examination. Follow these suggestions for maximum results from your efforts:

1) Cooperate with the monitor

The test administrator has a duty to create a situation in which you can be as much at ease as possible. He will give instructions, tell you when to begin, check to see that you are marking your answer sheet correctly, and so on. He is not there to guard you, although he will see that your competitors do not take unfair advantage. He wants to help you do your best.

2) Listen to all instructions

Don't jump the gun! Wait until you understand all directions. In most civil service tests you get more time than you need to answer the questions. So don't be in a hurry. Read each word of instructions until you clearly understand the meaning. Study the examples, listen to all announcements and follow directions. Ask questions if you do not understand what to do.

3) Identify your papers

Civil service exams are usually identified by number only. You will be assigned a number; you must not put your name on your test papers. Be sure to copy your number correctly. Since more than one exam may be given, copy your exact examination title.

4) Plan your time

Unless you are told that a test is a "speed" or "rate of work" test, speed itself is usually not important. Time enough to answer all the questions will be provided, but this does not mean that you have all day. An overall time limit has been set. Divide the total time (in minutes) by the number of questions to determine the approximate time you have for each question.

5) Do not linger over difficult questions

If you come across a difficult question, mark it with a paper clip (useful to have along) and come back to it when you have been through the booklet. One caution if you do this – be sure to skip a number on your answer sheet as well. Check often to be sure that you have not lost your place and that you are marking in the row numbered the same as the question you are answering.

6) Read the questions

Be sure you know what the question asks! Many capable people are unsuccessful because they failed to *read* the questions correctly.

7) Answer all questions

Unless you have been instructed that a penalty will be deducted for incorrect answers, it is better to guess than to omit a question.

8) Speed tests

It is often better NOT to guess on speed tests. It has been found that on timed tests people are tempted to spend the last few seconds before time is called in marking answers at random – without even reading them – in the hope of picking up a few extra points. To discourage this practice, the instructions may warn you that your score will be "corrected" for guessing. That is, a penalty will be applied. The incorrect answers will be deducted from the correct ones, or some other penalty formula will be used.

9) Review your answers

If you finish before time is called, go back to the questions you guessed or omitted to give them further thought. Review other answers if you have time.

10) Return your test materials

If you are ready to leave before others have finished or time is called, take ALL your materials to the monitor and leave quietly. Never take any test material with you. The monitor can discover whose papers are not complete, and taking a test booklet may be grounds for disqualification.

VIII. EXAMINATION TECHNIQUES

1) Read the general instructions carefully. These are usually printed on the first page of the exam booklet. As a rule, these instructions refer to the timing of the examination; the fact that you should not start work until the signal and must stop work at a signal, etc. If there are any *special* instructions, such as a choice of questions to be answered, make sure that you note this instruction carefully.

2) When you are ready to start work on the examination, that is as soon as the signal has been given, read the instructions to each question booklet, underline any key words or phrases, such as *least, best, outline, describe* and the like. In this way you will tend to answer as requested rather than discover on reviewing your paper that you *listed without describing*, that you selected the *worst* choice rather than the *best* choice, etc.

3) If the examination is of the objective or multiple-choice type – that is, each question will also give a series of possible answers: A, B, C or D, and you are called upon to select the best answer and write the letter next to that answer on your answer paper – it is advisable to start answering each question in turn. There may be anywhere from 50 to 100 such questions in the three or four hours allotted and you can see how much time would be taken if you read through all the questions before beginning to answer any. Furthermore, if you come across a question or group of questions which you know would be difficult to answer, it would undoubtedly affect your handling of all the other questions.

4) If the examination is of the essay type and contains but a few questions, it is a moot point as to whether you should read all the questions before starting to answer any one. Of course, if you are given a choice – say five out of seven and the like – then it is essential to read all the questions so you can eliminate the two that are most difficult. If, however, you are asked to answer all the questions, there may be danger in trying to answer the easiest one first because you may find that you will spend too much time on it. The best technique is to answer the first question, then proceed to the second, etc.

5) Time your answers. Before the exam begins, write down the time it started, then add the time allowed for the examination and write down the time it must be completed, then divide the time available somewhat as follows:
   - If 3-1/2 hours are allowed, that would be 210 minutes. If you have 80 objective-type questions, that would be an average of 2-1/2 minutes per question. Allow yourself no more than 2 minutes per question, or a total of 160 minutes, which will permit about 50 minutes to review.
   - If for the time allotment of 210 minutes there are 7 essay questions to answer, that would average about 30 minutes a question. Give yourself only 25 minutes per question so that you have about 35 minutes to review.

6) The most important instruction is to *read each question* and make sure you know what is wanted. The second most important instruction is to *time yourself properly* so that you answer every question. The third most important instruction is to *answer every question*. Guess if you have to but include something for each question. Remember that you will receive no credit for a blank and will probably receive some credit if you write something in answer to an essay question. If you guess a letter – say "B" for a multiple-choice question – you may have guessed right. If you leave a blank as an answer to a multiple-choice question, the examiners may respect your feelings but it will not add a point to your score. Some exams may penalize you for wrong answers, so in such cases *only*, you may not want to guess unless you have some basis for your answer.

7) Suggestions
   a. Objective-type questions
      1. Examine the question booklet for proper sequence of pages and questions
      2. Read all instructions carefully
      3. Skip any question which seems too difficult; return to it after all other questions have been answered
      4. Apportion your time properly; do not spend too much time on any single question or group of questions

5. Note and underline key words – *all, most, fewest, least, best, worst, same, opposite,* etc.
6. Pay particular attention to negatives
7. Note unusual option, e.g., unduly long, short, complex, different or similar in content to the body of the question
8. Observe the use of "hedging" words – *probably, may, most likely,* etc.
9. Make sure that your answer is put next to the same number as the question
10. Do not second-guess unless you have good reason to believe the second answer is definitely more correct
11. Cross out original answer if you decide another answer is more accurate; do not erase until you are ready to hand your paper in
12. Answer all questions; guess unless instructed otherwise
13. Leave time for review

b. Essay questions
1. Read each question carefully
2. Determine exactly what is wanted. Underline key words or phrases.
3. Decide on outline or paragraph answer
4. Include many different points and elements unless asked to develop any one or two points or elements
5. Show impartiality by giving pros and cons unless directed to select one side only
6. Make and write down any assumptions you find necessary to answer the questions
7. Watch your English, grammar, punctuation and choice of words
8. Time your answers; don't crowd material

8) Answering the essay question

Most essay questions can be answered by framing the specific response around several key words or ideas. Here are a few such key words or ideas:

M's: manpower, materials, methods, money, management
P's: purpose, program, policy, plan, procedure, practice, problems, pitfalls, personnel, public relations

a. Six basic steps in handling problems:
1. Preliminary plan and background development
2. Collect information, data and facts
3. Analyze and interpret information, data and facts
4. Analyze and develop solutions as well as make recommendations
5. Prepare report and sell recommendations
6. Install recommendations and follow up effectiveness

b. Pitfalls to avoid
1. *Taking things for granted* – A statement of the situation does not necessarily imply that each of the elements is necessarily true; for example, a complaint may be invalid and biased so that all that can be taken for granted is that a complaint has been registered

2. *Considering only one side of a situation* – Wherever possible, indicate several alternatives and then point out the reasons you selected the best one
3. *Failing to indicate follow up* – Whenever your answer indicates action on your part, make certain that you will take proper follow-up action to see how successful your recommendations, procedures or actions turn out to be
4. *Taking too long in answering any single question* – Remember to time your answers properly

IX. AFTER THE TEST

Scoring procedures differ in detail among civil service jurisdictions although the general principles are the same. Whether the papers are hand-scored or graded by machine we have described, they are nearly always graded by number. That is, the person who marks the paper knows only the number – never the name – of the applicant. Not until all the papers have been graded will they be matched with names. If other tests, such as training and experience or oral interview ratings have been given, scores will be combined. Different parts of the examination usually have different weights. For example, the written test might count 60 percent of the final grade, and a rating of training and experience 40 percent. In many jurisdictions, veterans will have a certain number of points added to their grades.

After the final grade has been determined, the names are placed in grade order and an eligible list is established. There are various methods for resolving ties between those who get the same final grade – probably the most common is to place first the name of the person whose application was received first. Job offers are made from the eligible list in the order the names appear on it. You will be notified of your grade and your rank as soon as all these computations have been made. This will be done as rapidly as possible.

People who are found to meet the requirements in the announcement are called "eligibles." Their names are put on a list of eligible candidates. An eligible's chances of getting a job depend on how high he stands on this list and how fast agencies are filling jobs from the list.

When a job is to be filled from a list of eligibles, the agency asks for the names of people on the list of eligibles for that job. When the civil service commission receives this request, it sends to the agency the names of the three people highest on this list. Or, if the job to be filled has specialized requirements, the office sends the agency the names of the top three persons who meet these requirements from the general list.

The appointing officer makes a choice from among the three people whose names were sent to him. If the selected person accepts the appointment, the names of the others are put back on the list to be considered for future openings.

That is the rule in hiring from all kinds of eligible lists, whether they are for typist, carpenter, chemist, or something else. For every vacancy, the appointing officer has his choice of any one of the top three eligibles on the list. This explains why the person whose name is on top of the list sometimes does not get an appointment when some of the persons lower on the list do. If the appointing officer chooses the second or third eligible, the No. 1 eligible does not get a job at once, but stays on the list until he is appointed or the list is terminated.

X. HOW TO PASS THE INTERVIEW TEST

The examination for which you applied requires an oral interview test. You have already taken the written test and you are now being called for the interview test – the final part of the formal examination.

You may think that it is not possible to prepare for an interview test and that there are no procedures to follow during an interview. Our purpose is to point out some things you can do in advance that will help you and some good rules to follow and pitfalls to avoid while you are being interviewed.

What is an interview supposed to test?

The written examination is designed to test the technical knowledge and competence of the candidate; the oral is designed to evaluate intangible qualities, not readily measured otherwise, and to establish a list showing the relative fitness of each candidate – as measured against his competitors – for the position sought. Scoring is not on the basis of "right" and "wrong," but on a sliding scale of values ranging from "not passable" to "outstanding." As a matter of fact, it is possible to achieve a relatively low score without a single "incorrect" answer because of evident weakness in the qualities being measured.

Occasionally, an examination may consist entirely of an oral test – either an individual or a group oral. In such cases, information is sought concerning the technical knowledges and abilities of the candidate, since there has been no written examination for this purpose. More commonly, however, an oral test is used to supplement a written examination.

Who conducts interviews?

The composition of oral boards varies among different jurisdictions. In nearly all, a representative of the personnel department serves as chairman. One of the members of the board may be a representative of the department in which the candidate would work. In some cases, "outside experts" are used, and, frequently, a businessman or some other representative of the general public is asked to serve. Labor and management or other special groups may be represented. The aim is to secure the services of experts in the appropriate field.

However the board is composed, it is a good idea (and not at all improper or unethical) to ascertain in advance of the interview who the members are and what groups they represent. When you are introduced to them, you will have some idea of their backgrounds and interests, and at least you will not stutter and stammer over their names.

What should be done before the interview?

While knowledge about the board members is useful and takes some of the surprise element out of the interview, there is other preparation which is more substantive. It *is* possible to prepare for an oral interview – in several ways:

1) Keep a copy of your application and review it carefully before the interview

This may be the only document before the oral board, and the starting point of the interview. Know what education and experience you have listed there, and the sequence and dates of all of it. Sometimes the board will ask you to review the highlights of your experience for them; you should not have to hem and haw doing it.

2) Study the class specification and the examination announcement

Usually, the oral board has one or both of these to guide them. The qualities, characteristics or knowledges required by the position sought are stated in these documents. They offer valuable clues as to the nature of the oral interview. For example, if the job involves supervisory responsibilities, the announcement will usually indicate that knowledge of modern supervisory methods and the qualifications of the candidate as a supervisor will be tested. If so, you can expect such questions, frequently in the form of a hypothetical situation which you are expected to solve. NEVER go into an oral without knowledge of the duties and responsibilities of the job you seek.

3) Think through each qualification required

Try to visualize the kind of questions you would ask if you were a board member. How well could you answer them? Try especially to appraise your own knowledge and background in each area, *measured against the job sought*, and identify any areas in which you are weak. Be critical and realistic – do not flatter yourself.

4) Do some general reading in areas in which you feel you may be weak

For example, if the job involves supervision and your past experience has NOT, some general reading in supervisory methods and practices, particularly in the field of human relations, might be useful. Do NOT study agency procedures or detailed manuals. The oral board will be testing your understanding and capacity, not your memory.

5) Get a good night's sleep and watch your general health and mental attitude

You will want a clear head at the interview. Take care of a cold or any other minor ailment, and of course, no hangovers.

What should be done on the day of the interview?

Now comes the day of the interview itself. Give yourself plenty of time to get there. Plan to arrive somewhat ahead of the scheduled time, particularly if your appointment is in the fore part of the day. If a previous candidate fails to appear, the board might be ready for you a bit early. By early afternoon an oral board is almost invariably behind schedule if there are many candidates, and you may have to wait. Take along a book or magazine to read, or your application to review, but leave any extraneous material in the waiting room when you go in for your interview. In any event, relax and compose yourself.

The matter of dress is important. The board is forming impressions about you – from your experience, your manners, your attitude, and your appearance. Give your personal appearance careful attention. Dress your best, but not your flashiest. Choose conservative, appropriate clothing, and be sure it is immaculate. This is a business interview, and your appearance should indicate that you regard it as such. Besides, being well groomed and properly dressed will help boost your confidence.

Sooner or later, someone will call your name and escort you into the interview room. *This is it.* From here on you are on your own. It is too late for any more preparation. But remember, you asked for this opportunity to prove your fitness, and you are here because your request was granted.

What happens when you go in?

The usual sequence of events will be as follows: The clerk (who is often the board stenographer) will introduce you to the chairman of the oral board, who will introduce you to the other members of the board. Acknowledge the introductions before you sit down. Do not be surprised if you find a microphone facing you or a stenotypist sitting by. Oral interviews are usually recorded in the event of an appeal or other review.

Usually the chairman of the board will open the interview by reviewing the highlights of your education and work experience from your application – primarily for the benefit of the other members of the board, as well as to get the material into the record. Do not interrupt or comment unless there is an error or significant misinterpretation; if that is the case, do not hesitate. But do not quibble about insignificant matters. Also, he will usually ask you some question about your education, experience or your present job – partly to get you to start talking and to establish the interviewing "rapport." He may start the actual questioning, or turn it over to one of the other members. Frequently, each member undertakes the questioning on a particular area, one in which he is perhaps most competent, so you can expect each member to participate in the examination. Because time is limited, you may also expect some rather abrupt switches in the direction the questioning takes, so do not be upset by it. Normally, a board member will not pursue a single line of questioning unless he discovers a particular strength or weakness.

After each member has participated, the chairman will usually ask whether any member has any further questions, then will ask you if you have anything you wish to add. Unless you are expecting this question, it may floor you. Worse, it may start you off on an extended, extemporaneous speech. The board is not usually seeking more information. The question is principally to offer you a last opportunity to present further qualifications or to indicate that you have nothing to add. So, if you feel that a significant qualification or characteristic has been overlooked, it is proper to point it out in a sentence or so. Do not compliment the board on the thoroughness of their examination – they have been sketchy, and you know it. If you wish, merely say, "No thank you, I have nothing further to add." This is a point where you can "talk yourself out" of a good impression or fail to present an important bit of information. Remember, *you close the interview yourself.*

The chairman will then say, "That is all, Mr. ______, thank you." Do not be startled; the interview is over, and quicker than you think. Thank him, gather your belongings and take your leave. Save your sigh of relief for the other side of the door.

How to put your best foot forward

Throughout this entire process, you may feel that the board individually and collectively is trying to pierce your defenses, seek out your hidden weaknesses and embarrass and confuse you. Actually, this is not true. They are obliged to make an appraisal of your qualifications for the job you are seeking, and they want to see you in your best light. Remember, they must interview all candidates and a non-cooperative candidate may become a failure in spite of their best efforts to bring out his qualifications. Here are 15 suggestions that will help you:

1) Be natural – Keep your attitude confident, not cocky

If you are not confident that you can do the job, do not expect the board to be. Do not apologize for your weaknesses, try to bring out your strong points. The board is interested in a positive, not negative, presentation. Cockiness will antagonize any board member and make him wonder if you are covering up a weakness by a false show of strength.

2) Get comfortable, but don't lounge or sprawl

Sit erectly but not stiffly. A careless posture may lead the board to conclude that you are careless in other things, or at least that you are not impressed by the importance of the occasion. Either conclusion is natural, even if incorrect. Do not fuss with your clothing, a pencil or an ashtray. Your hands may occasionally be useful to emphasize a point; do not let them become a point of distraction.

3) Do not wisecrack or make small talk

This is a serious situation, and your attitude should show that you consider it as such. Further, the time of the board is limited – they do not want to waste it, and neither should you.

4) Do not exaggerate your experience or abilities

In the first place, from information in the application or other interviews and sources, the board may know more about you than you think. Secondly, you probably will not get away with it. An experienced board is rather adept at spotting such a situation, so do not take the chance.

5) If you know a board member, do not make a point of it, yet do not hide it

Certainly you are not fooling him, and probably not the other members of the board. Do not try to take advantage of your acquaintanceship – it will probably do you little good.

6) Do not dominate the interview

Let the board do that. They will give you the clues – do not assume that you have to do all the talking. Realize that the board has a number of questions to ask you, and do not try to take up all the interview time by showing off your extensive knowledge of the answer to the first one.

7) Be attentive

You only have 20 minutes or so, and you should keep your attention at its sharpest throughout. When a member is addressing a problem or question to you, give him your undivided attention. Address your reply principally to him, but do not exclude the other board members.

8) Do not interrupt

A board member may be stating a problem for you to analyze. He will ask you a question when the time comes. Let him state the problem, and wait for the question.

9) Make sure you understand the question

Do not try to answer until you are sure what the question is. If it is not clear, restate it in your own words or ask the board member to clarify it for you. However, do not haggle about minor elements.

10) Reply promptly but not hastily

A common entry on oral board rating sheets is "candidate responded readily," or "candidate hesitated in replies." Respond as promptly and quickly as you can, but do not jump to a hasty, ill-considered answer.

11) Do not be peremptory in your answers

A brief answer is proper – but do not fire your answer back. That is a losing game from your point of view. The board member can probably ask questions much faster than you can answer them.

12) Do not try to create the answer you think the board member wants

He is interested in what kind of mind you have and how it works – not in playing games. Furthermore, he can usually spot this practice and will actually grade you down on it.

13) Do not switch sides in your reply merely to agree with a board member

Frequently, a member will take a contrary position merely to draw you out and to see if you are willing and able to defend your point of view. Do not start a debate, yet do not surrender a good position. If a position is worth taking, it is worth defending.

14) Do not be afraid to admit an error in judgment if you are shown to be wrong

The board knows that you are forced to reply without any opportunity for careful consideration. Your answer may be demonstrably wrong. If so, admit it and get on with the interview.

15) Do not dwell at length on your present job

The opening question may relate to your present assignment. Answer the question but do not go into an extended discussion. You are being examined for a *new* job, not your present one. As a matter of fact, try to phrase ALL your answers in terms of the job for which you are being examined.

Basis of Rating

Probably you will forget most of these "do's" and "don'ts" when you walk into the oral interview room. Even remembering them all will not ensure you a passing grade. Perhaps you did not have the qualifications in the first place. But remembering them will help you to put your best foot forward, without treading on the toes of the board members.

Rumor and popular opinion to the contrary notwithstanding, an oral board wants you to make the best appearance possible. They know you are under pressure – but they also want to see how you respond to it as a guide to what your reaction would be under the pressures of the job you seek. They will be influenced by the degree of poise you display, the personal traits you show and the manner in which you respond.

ABOUT THIS BOOK

This book contains tests divided into Examination Sections. Go through each test, answering every question in the margin. We have also attached a sample answer sheet at the back of the book that can be removed and used. At the end of each test look at the answer key and check your answers. On the ones you got wrong, look at the right answer choice and learn. Do not fill in the answers first. Do not memorize the questions and answers, but understand the answer and principles involved. On your test, the questions will likely be different from the samples. Questions are changed and new ones added. If you understand these past questions you should have success with any changes that arise. Tests may consist of several types of questions. We have additional books on each subject should more study be advisable or necessary for you. Finally, the more you study, the better prepared you will be. This book is intended to be the last thing you study before you walk into the examination room. Prior study of relevant texts is also recommended. NLC publishes some of these in our Fundamental Series. Knowledge and good sense are important factors in passing your exam. Good luck also helps. So now study this Passbook, absorb the material contained within and take that knowledge into the examination. Then do your best to pass that exam.

EXAMINATION SECTION

EXAMINATION SECTION
TEST 1

DIRECTIONS: Each question or incomplete statement is followed by several suggested answers or completions. Select the one that BEST answers the question or completes the statement. *PRINT THE LETTER OF THE CORRECT ANSWER IN THE SPACE AT THE RIGHT.*

1. When you select someone to serve as supervisor of your unit during your absence on vacation and at other times, it would generally be BEST to choose the employee who is 1.____

   A. able to move the work along smoothly without friction
   B. on staff longest
   C. liked best by the rest of the staff
   D. able to perform the work of each employee to be supervised

2. Successful supervision of handicapped persons employed in a department depends MOST on providing them with a work place and work climate 2.____

   A. which is safe and accident-free
   B. that requires close and direct supervision by others
   C. that requires the performance of routine, repetitive tasks under a minimum of pressure
   D. where they will be accepted by the other employees

3. Studies have indicated that when employees feel that their work is aimless and unchallenging, the allocation or payment of more money for this type of work is LIKELY to 3.____

   A. contribute little to increased production
   B. bring more status to this work
   C. increase employees' feelings of security
   D. give employees greater motivation

4. An employee's performance has fallen below established minimum standards of quantity and quality. 4.____
   The threat of monetary or other disciplinary action as a device for improving this employee's performance would PROBABLY be acceptable and most effective

   A. only if applied as soon as the performance fell below standard
   B. only after more constructive techniques have failed
   C. at any time provided the employee understands that the punishment will be carried out
   D. at no time

5. A supervisor must, on short notice, ask his staff to work overtime. 5.____
   Of the following, a technique that is MOST likely to win their willing cooperation would be to

   A. explain that occasional overtime is part of the job requirement
   B. explain that they will be doing him a personal favor which he will appreciate very much
   C. explain why the overtime is necessary
   D. promise them that they can take the extra time off in the near future

6. On checking a completed work assignment of an employee, the supervisor finds that the work was not done correctly because the employee had not understood his instructions. Of the following, the BEST way to prevent repetition of this situation next time is for the supervisor to 6.____

A. ask the employee whether he fully understood the instructions and tell him to ask questions in the future whenever anything is unclear
B. ask the employee to repeat the instructions given and test his understanding with several key questions
C. give the instructions a second time, emphasizing the more complicated aspects of the job
D. give work instructions in writing

7. If, as a supervisor, you find yourself pressured for time to handle all of your job responsibilities, the one of the following tasks which it would be MOST appropriate for you to delegate to a subordinate is 7.____

A. attending a staff conference of unit supervisors to discuss the implementation of a new departmental policy
B. making staff work assignments
C. interviewing a new employee
D. checking work of certain employees for accuracy

8. Suppose you are unavoidably late for work one morning. When you arrive at 10 o'clock, you find there are several matters demanding your attention. 8.____
Which one of the following matters should you handle LAST?

A. A visitor who had a 9:30 appointment with you has been waiting to see you since 9 o'clock
B. An employee on an assignment which should have been completed that morning is absent, and the work will have to be reassigned
C. Several letters which you dictated at the end of the previous day have been typed and are on your desk for signature and mailing
D. Your superior called asking you to get certain information for him when you come in and to call him back

9. Suppose that you have assigned a typist to type a report containing considerable statistical and tabular material and have given her specific instructions as to how this material is to be laid out on each page. When she returns the completed report, you find that it was not prepared according to your instructions, but you may possibly be able to use it the way it was typed. When you question her, she states that she thought her layout was better, but you were unavailable for consultation when she began the work. 9.____
Of the following, the BEST action for you to take is to

A. criticize her for not doing the work according to your instructions
B. have her retype the report
C. praise her for her work but tell her she could have waited until she could consult you
D. praise her for using initiative

10. Of the following, the MOST effective way for a supervisor to correct poor working habits of an employee which result in low and poor quality output is to give the employee 10.____

A. additional training
B. less demanding assignments until his work improves
C. continuous supervision
D. more severe criticism

11. Of the following, the BEST way for a supervisor to teach an employee how to do a new and somewhat complicated job is to 11.____

A. assign him to observe another employee who is already skilled in this work and instruct him to consult this employee if he has any questions
B. explain to him how to do it, then demonstrate how it is done, then observe and correct the employee as he does it, then follow up
C. give him a written, detailed, step-by-step explanation of how to do the job and instruct him to ask questions if anything is unclear when he does the work
D. teach him the easiest part of the job first, then the other parts one at a time, in order of their difficulty, as the employee masters the easier parts

12. After an employee has completed telling his supervisor about a grievance against a co-worker, the supervisor tells the employee that he will take action to remove the cause of the grievance. 12.____
The action of the supervisor was

A. *good* because ill feeling between subordinates interferes with proper performance
B. *poor* because the supervisor should give both employees time to *cool off*
C. *good* because grievances that appear petty to the supervisor are important to subordinates
D. *poor* because the supervisor should tell the employee that he will investigate the matter before he comes to any conclusion

13. During work on an important project, one employee in a secretarial pool turns in several pages of typed copy, one page of which contains several errors. 13.____
Of these four comments which her supervisor might possibly make, which one would be MOST constructive?

A. "You did such a poor job on this; I 'll have to have it done over."
B. "You will have to do better more consistently than this if you want to be in charge of a secretarial pool yourself someday."
C. "How come you made so many mistakes here? Your other pages were all right."
D. "If my boss saw this, he'd be very displeased with you."

14. A supervisor has general supervision over a large, complex project with many employees. The work is subdivided among small units of employees, each with a senior clerk or senior stenographer in charge. At a staff meeting, after all work assignments have been made, the supervisor tells all the employees that they are to take orders only from their immediate supervisor and instructs them to let him know if any one else tries to give them orders. 14.____
This instruction by the supervisor is

A. *good* because it may prevent the issuance of orders by unauthorized persons which would interfere with the accomplishment of the assignment
B. *poor* because employees should be instructed to take up such problems with their immediate supervisor

C. *good* because orders issued by immediate supervisors would be precise and directly related to the tasks of the assignments while those issued by others would not be
D. *poor* because it places upon all employees a responsibility which should not normally be theirs

15. A supervisor who is to direct a team of senior clerks and clerks and senior stenographers and stenographers in a complex project calls them together beforehand to inform them of the tasks each employee will perform on this job. Of the following, the CHIEF value of this action by the supervisor is that each member of this team will be able to 15.____

A. work independently in the absence of the supervisor
B. understand what he will do and how this will fit into the total picture
C. share in the process of decision-making as an equal participant
D. judge how well the plans for this assignment have been made

16. A supervisor who has both younger and older employees under his supervision may sometimes find that employee absenteeism seriously interferes with accomplishment of goals. 16.____
Studies of such employee absenteeism have shown that the absences of employees

A. under 35 years of age are usually unexpected and the absences of employees over 45 years of age are usually unnecessary
B. of all age groups show the same characteristics as to length of absence
C. under 35 years of age are for frequent, short periods while the absences of employees over 45 years of age are less frequent but of longer duration
D. under 35 years of age are for periods of long duration and the absences of employees over 45 years of age are for periods of short duration

17. Suppose you have a long-standing procedure for getting a certain job done by your subordinates that is apparently a good one. Changes in some steps of the procedure are made from time to time to handle special problems that come up. 17.____
For you to review this procedure periodically is desirable MAINLY because

A. the system is working well
B. checking routines periodically is a supervisor's chief responsibility
C. subordinates may be confused as to how the procedure operates as a result of the changes made
D. it is necessary to determine whether the procedure has become outdated or is in need of improvement

18. In conducting an interview, the BEST types of questions with which to begin the interview are those which the person interviewed is ______ to answer. 18.____

A. willing and able
B. willing but unable
C. able to but unwilling
D. unable and unwilling

19. In order to determine accurately a child's age, it is BEST for an interviewer to rely on 19.____

A. the child's grade in school
B. what the mother says
C. birth records
D. a library card

20. In his first interview with a new employee, it would be LEAST appropriate for a unit supervisor to 20.____

A. find out the employee's preference for the several types of jobs to which he is able to assign him
B. determine whether the employee will make good promotion material
C. inform the employee of what his basic job responsibilities will be
D. inquire about the employee's education and previous employment

21. If an interviewer takes care to phrase his questions carefully and precisely, the result will MOST probably be that 21.____

A. he will be able to determine whether the person interviewed is being truthful
B. the free flow of the interview will be lost
C. he will get the information he wants
D. he will ask stereotyped questions and narrow the scope of the interview

22. When, during an interview, is the person interviewed LEAST likely to be cautious about what he tells the interviewer? 22.____

A. Shortly after the beginning when the questions normally suggest pleasant associations to the person interviewed
B. As long as the interviewer keeps his questions to the point
C. At the point where the person interviewed gains a clear insight into the area being discussed
D. When the interview appears formally ended and goodbyes are being said

23. In an interview held for the purpose of getting information from the person interviewed, it is sometimes desirable for the interviewer to repeat the answer he has received to a question. 23.____
For the interviewer to rephrase such an answer in his own words is good practice MAINLY because it

A. gives the interviewer time to make up his next question
B. gives the person interviewed a chance to correct any possible misunderstanding
C. gives the person interviewed the feeling that the interviewer considers his answer important
D. prevents the person interviewed from changing his answer

24. There are several methods of formulating questions during an interview. The particular method used should be adapted to the interview problems presented by the person being questioned. 24.____
Of the following methods of formulating questions during an interview, the ACCEPTABLE one is for the interviewer to ask questions which

A. incorporate several items in order to allow a cooperative interviewee freedom to organize his statements
B. are ambiguous in order to foil a distrustful interviewee
C. suggest the correct answer in order to assist an interviewee who appears confused
D. would help an otherwise unresponsive interviewee to become more responsive

25. For an interviewer to permit the person being interviewed to read the data the interviewer writes as he records the person's responses on a routine departmental form is 25.___

A. *desirable* because it serves to assure the person interviewed that his responses are being recorded accurately
B. *undesirable* because it prevents the interviewer from clarifying uncertain points by asking additional questions
C. *desirable* because it makes the time that the person interviewed must wait while the answer is written seem shorter
D. *undesirable* because it destroys the confidentiality of the interview

26. Suppose that a stranger enters the office you are in charge of and asks for the address and telephone number of one of your employees. 26.___
Of the following, it would be BEST for you to

A. find out why he needs the information and release it if his reason is a good one
B. explain that you are not permitted to release such information to unauthorized persons
C. give him the information but tell him it must be kept confidential
D. ask him to leave the office immediately

27. A member of the public approaches an employee who is at work at his desk. The employee cannot interrupt his work in order to take care of this person. 27.___
Of the following, the BEST and MOST courteous way of handling this situation is for the employee to

A. avoid looking up from his work until he is finished with what he is doing
B. tell this person that he will not be able to take care of him for quite a while
C. refer the individual to another employee who can take care of him right away
D. chat with the individual while he continues with his work

28. You answer a phone call from a citizen who urgently needs certain information you do not have, but you think you know who may have it. He is angry because he has already been switched to two different offices. 28.___
Of the following, it would be BEST for you to

A. give him the phone number of the person you think may have the information he wants, but explain you are not sure
B. tell him you regret you cannot help him because you are not sure who can give him the information
C. advise him that the best way he can be sure of getting the information he wants is to write a letter to the agency
D. get the phone number where he can be reached and tell him you will try to get the information he wants and will call him back later

29. Persons who have business with an agency often complain about the *red tape* which complicates or slows up what they are trying to accomplish. 29.___
As a supervisor of a unit which deals with the public, the LEAST effective of the following actions which you could take to counteract this feeling on the part of a person who has business with your office is to

A. assure him that your office will make every effort to take care of his matter as fast as possible
B. tell him that because of the volume of work in your agency he must be patient with *red tape*

C. give him a reasonable date by which action on the matter he is concerned about will be completed and tell him to call you if he hasn't heard by then
D. give him an understanding of why the procedures he must comply with are necessary

30. If a receptionist is sorting letters at her desk and a caller appears to make an inquiry, the receptionist should 30.____

A. ask the caller to have a seat and wait
B. speak to the caller while continuing the sorting, looking up occasionally
C. stop what she is doing and give undivided attention to the caller
D. continue with the sorting until a logical break in the work is reached, then answer any inquiries

31. To avoid cutting off parts of letters when using an automatic letter opener, it is BEST to 31.____

A. arrange all of the letters so that the addresses are right side up
B. hold the envelopes up to the light to make sure their contents have not settled to the side that is to be opened
C. strike the envelopes against a table or desk top several times so that the contents of all the envelopes settle to one side
D. check the enclosures periodically to make sure that the machine has not been cutting into them

32. Requests to repair office equipment which appears to be unsafe should be given priority MAINLY because if repairs are delayed 32.____

A. there may be injuries to staff
B. there may be further deterioration of the equipment
C. work flow may be interrupted
D. the cost of repair may increase

33. Of the following types of documents, it is MOST important to retain and file 33.____

A. working drafts of reports that have been submitted in final form
B. copies of letters of good will which conveyed a message that could not be handled by phone
C. interoffice orders for materials which have been received and verified
D. interoffice memoranda regarding the routing of standard forms

34. Of the following, the BEST reason for discarding certain material from office files would be that the 34.____

A. files are crowded
B. material in the files is old
C. material duplicates information obtainable from other sources in the files
D. material is referred to most often by employees in an adjoining office

35. Of the following, the BEST reason for setting up a partitioned work area for the typists in your office is that 35.____

A. an uninterrupted flow of work among the typists will be possible
B. complaints about ventilation and lighting will be reduced
C. the first-line supervisor will have more direct control over the typists
D. the noise of the typewriters will be less disturbing to other workers

36. Of the following, the MAIN factor contributing to the expense of maintaining an office procedure manual would be the 36.___

A. infrequent use of the manual
B. need to revise it regularly
C. cost of looseleaf binders
D. high cost of printing

37. From the viewpoint of use of a typewriter to fill in a form, the MOST important design factor to consider is 37.___

A. standard spacing
B. box headings
C. serial numbering
D. vertical guide lines

38. Out-of-date and seldom used records should be removed PERIODICALLY from the files because 38.___

A. overall responsibility for records will be transferred to the person in charge of the central storage files
B. duplicate copies of every record are not needed
C. valuable filing space will be regained and the time needed to find a current record will be cut down
D. worthwhile suggestions on improving the filing system will result whenever this is done

39. In a certain office, file folders are constantly being removed from the files for use by administrators. At the same time, new material is coming in to be filed in some of these folders. 39.___
Of the following, the BEST way to avoid delays in filing of the new material and to keep track of the removed folders is to

A. keep a sheet listing all folders removed from the file, who has them, and a follow-up date to check on their return; attach to this list new material received for filing
B. put an *out* slip in the place of any file folder removed, telling what folder is missing, date removed, and who has it; file new material received at front of files
C. put a temporary *out* folder in place of the one removed, giving title or subject, date removed, and who has it; put into this temporary folder any new material received
D. keep a list of all folders removed and who has them; forward any new material received for filing while a folder is out to the person who has it

40. Folders labeled *Miscellaneous* should be used in an alphabetic filing system MAINLY to 40.___

A. provide quick access to recent material
B. avoid setting up individual folders for all infrequent correspondents
C. provide temporary storage for less important documents
D. temporarily hold papers which will not fit into already crowded individual folders

41. Suppose that one of the office machines in your unit is badly in need of replacement. Of the following, the MOST important reason for postponing immediate purchase of a new machine would be that 41.___

A. a later model of the machine is expected on the market in a few months
B. the new machine is more expensive than the old machine
C. the operator of the present machine will have to be instructed by the manufacturer in the operation of the new machine
D. the employee operating the old machine is not complaining

42. If the four steps listed below for processing records were given in logical sequence, the one that would be the THIRD step is: 42.____

A. Coding the records, using a chart or classification system
B. Inspecting the records to make sure they have been released for filing
C. Preparing cross-reference sheets or cards
D. Skimming the records to determine filing captions

43. The suggestion that memos or directives which circulate among subordinates be initialed by each employee is a 43.____

A. *poor* one because, with modern copying machines, it should be possible to supply every subordinate with a copy of each message for his personal use
B. *good* one because it relieves the supervisor of blame for the action of subordinates who have read and initialed the messages
C. *poor* one because initialing the memo or directive is no guarantee that the subordinate has read the material
D. *good* one because it can be used as a record by the supervisor to show that his subordinates have received the message and were responsible for reading it

44. Of the following, the MOST important reason for microfilming office records is to 44.____

A. save storage space needed to keep records
B. make it easier to get records when needed
C. speed up the classification of information
D. shorten the time which records must be kept

45. Your office filing cabinets have become so overcrowded that it is difficult to use the files. Of the following, the MOST desirable step for you to take FIRST to relieve this situation would be to 45.____

A. assign your assistant to spend some time each day reviewing the material in the files and to give you his recommendations as to what material may be discarded
B. discard all material which has been in the files more than a given number of years
C. submit a request for additional filing cabinets in your next budget request
D. transfer enough material to the central storage room of your agency to give you the amount of additional filing space needed

46. Of the following, the USUAL order of the subdivisions in a standard published report is: 46.____

A. Table of contents, body of report, index, appendix
B. Index, table of contents, body of report, appendix
C. Index, body of report, table of contents, appendix
D. Table of contents, body of report, appendix, index

47. The BEST type of pictorial illustration to show the approximate percentage breakdown of the titles of employees in a department would be the 47.____

A. flow chart
B. bar graph
C. organization chart
D. line graph

48. You are reviewing a draft, written by one of your subordinates, of a report that is to be distributed to every bureau and division of your department. 48.___
Which one of the following would be the LEAST desirable characteristic of such a report?

A. It gives information, explanations, conclusions, and recommendations for which purpose it was written.
B. There is sufficient objective data presented to substantiate the conclusions reached and the recommendations made by the writer.
C. The writing style and opinions of the writer are persuasive enough to win over to its conclusions those who read the report, although little data is given in support.
D. It will be understood easily by the people to whom it will be distributed.

49. According to accepted practice, a business letter is addressed to an organization but marked for the attention of a specific individual whenever the sender wants 49.___

A. only the person to whose attention the letter is sent to read the letter
B. the letter to be opened and taken care of by someone else in the organization of the person for whose attention it is marked is away
C. a reply only from the specific individual
D. to improve the appearance and balance of the letter in cases where the company address is a long one

50. Which one of the following would be an ACCEPTABLE way to end a business letter? 50.___

A. Hoping you will find this information useful, I remain
B. Yours for continuing service
C. I hope this letter gives you the information you need
D. Trusting this gives you the information you desire, I am

KEY (CORRECT ANSWERS)

1. A	11. B	21. C	31. C	41. A
2. D	12. D	22. D	32. A	42. A
3. A	13. C	23. B	33. D	43. D
4. B	14. B	24. D	34. C	44. A
5. C	15. B	25. A	35. D	45. A
6. B	16. C	26. B	36. B	46. D
7. D	17. D	27. C	37. A	47. B
8. C	18. A	28. D	38. C	48. C
9. A	19. C	29. B	39. C	49. B
10. A	20. B	30. C	40. B	50. C

TEST 2

DIRECTIONS: Each question or incomplete statement is followed by several suggested answers or completions. Select the one that BEST answers the question or completes the statement. *PRINT THE LETTER OF THE CORRECT ANSWER IN THE SPACE AT THE RIGHT.*

1. You are replying to a letter from an individual who asks for a pamphlet put out by your agency. The pamphlet is out of print. A new pamphlet with a different title, but dealing with the same subject, is available. 1.____
   Of the following, it would be BEST that your reply indicate that

   A. you cannot send him the pamphlet he requested because it is out of print
   B. the pamphlet he requested is out of print, but he may be able to find it in the public library
   C. the pamphlet he requested is out of print, but you are sending him a copy of your agency's new pamphlet on the same subject
   D. since the pamphlet he requested is out of print, you would advise him to ask his friends or business acquaintances if they have a copy of it

2. An angry citizen sends a letter to your agency claiming that your office sent him the wrong form and complaining about the general inefficiency of city workers. Upon checking, you find that an incorrect form was indeed sent to this person. 2.____
   In reply, you should

   A. admit the error, apologize briefly, and enclose the correct form
   B. send the citizen the correct form with a transmittal letter stating only that the form is enclosed
   C. send him the correct form without any comment
   D. advise the citizen that mistakes happen in every large organization and that you are enclosing the correct form

3. It has been suggested that the language level of a letter of reply written by a government employee be geared no higher than the probable educational level of the person to whom the letter is written. 3.____
   This suggestion is a

   A. *good* one because it is easier for anyone to write letters simply, and this will make for a better reply
   B. *poor* one because it is not possible to judge, from one letter, the exact educational level of the writer
   C. *good* one because it will contribute to the recipient's comprehension of the contents of the letter
   D. *poor* one because the language should be at the simplest possible level so that anyone who reads the letter can understand it

4. Suppose that a large bureau has 187 employees. On a particular day, approximately 14% of these employees are not available for work because of absences due to vacation, illness, or other reasons. Of the remaining employees, 1/7 are assigned to a special project while the balance are assigned to the normal work of the bureau. 4.____
   The number of employees assigned to the normal work of the bureau on that day is

   A. 112　　B. 124　　C. 138　　D. 142

5. Suppose that you are in charge of a typing pool of 8 typists. Two typists type at the rate of 38 words per minute; three type at the rate of 40 words per minute; three type at the rate of 42 words per minute. The average typewritten page consists of 50 lines, 12 words per line. Each employee works from 9 to 5 with one hour off for lunch. 5.____
The total number of pages typed by this pool in one day is, on the average, CLOSEST to ______ pages.

A. 205 B. 225 C. 250 D. 275

6. Suppose that part-time workers are paid $14.40 an hour, prorated to the nearest half hour, with pay guaranteed for a minimum of four hours if services are required for less than four hours. In one operation, part-time workers signed the time sheet as follows: 6.____

Worker	In	Out
A	8:00 A.M.	11:35 A.M.
B	8:30 A.M.	3:20 P.M.
C	7:55 A.M.	11:00 A.M.
D	8:30 A.M.	2:25 P.M.

How much would total payment to these part-time workers amount to for this operation, assuming that those who stayed after 12 Noon were not paid for one hour which they took off for lunch?

A. $268.80 B. $273.60 C. $284.40 D. $297.60

7. He wanted to *ascertain* the facts before arriving at a conclusion. 7.____
The word *ascertain* means MOST NEARLY

A. disprove B. determine C. convert D. provide

8. Did the supervisor *assent* to her request for annual leave? The word *assent* means MOST NEARLY 8.____

A. allude B. protest C. agree D. refer

9. The new worker was fearful that the others would *rebuff* her. 9.____
The word *rebuff* means MOST NEARLY

A. ignore B. forget C. copy D. snub

10. The supervisor of that office does not *condone* lateness. The word *condone* means MOST NEARLY 10.____

A. mind B. excuse C. punish D. remember

11. Each employee was instructed to be as *concise* as possible when preparing a report. 11.____
The word *concise* means MOST NEARLY

A. exact B. sincere C. flexible D. brief

Questions 12-21.

DIRECTIONS: Below are 10 sentences numbered 12 to 21. Some of the sentences contain an error in spelling, word usage, or sentence structure, or punctuation. Some sentences are correct as they stand, although there may be other correct ways of expressing the same thought. All incorrect sentences contain only one error. Mark your answer to each question as follows:

A. if the sentence has an error in spelling
B. if the sentence has an error in punctuation or capitalization
C. if the sentence has an error in word usage or sentence structure
D. if the sentence is correct

12. Because the chairman failed to keep the participants from wandering off into irrelevant discussions, it was impossible to reach a consensus before the meeting was adjourned. 12.____

13. Certain employers have an unwritten rule that any applicant, who is over 55 years of age, is automatically excluded from consideration for any position whatsoever. 13.____

14. If the proposal to build schools in some new apartment buildings were to be accepted by the builders, one of the advantages that could be expected to result would be better communication between teachers and parents of schoolchildren. 14.____

15. In this instance, the manufacturer's violation of the law against deseptive packaging was discernible only to an experienced inspector. 15.____

16. The tenants' anger stemmed from the president's going to Washington to testify without consulting them first. 16.____

17. Did the president of this eminent banking company say; "We intend to hire and train a number of these disad-vantaged youths?" 17.____

18. In addition, today's confidential secretary must be knowledgable in many different areas: for example, she must know modern techniques for making travel arrangements for the executive. 18.____

19. To avoid further disruption of work in the offices, the protesters were forbidden from entering the building unless they had special passes. 19.____

20. A valuable secondary result of our training conferences is the opportunities afforded for management to observe the reactions of the participants. 20.____

21. Of the two proposals submitted by the committee, the first one is the best. 21.____

Questions 22-26.

DIRECTIONS: In Questions 22 through 26, choose the sentence which is BEST from the point of view of English usage suitable for a business letter or report.

22. 22.____
A. It is the opinion of the Commissioners that programs which include the construction of cut-rate municipal garages in the central business district is inadvisable.
B. Having reviewed the material submitted, the program for putting up cut-rate garages in the central business district seemed likely to cause traffic congestion.
C. The Commissioners believe that putting up cut-rate municipal garages in the central business district is inadvisable.
D. Making an effort to facilitate the cleaning of streets in the central business district, the building of cut-rate municipal garages presents the problem that it would encourage more motorists to come into the central city.

23. A. This letter, together with the reports, are to be sent to the principal. 23.____
B. The reports, together with this letter, is to be sent to the principal.
C. The reports and this letter is to be sent to the principal.
D. This letter, together with the reports, is to be sent to the principal.

24. A. Each employee has to decide for themselves whether to take the examination. 24.____
B. Each of the employees has to decide for himself whether to take the examination.
C. Each of the employees has to decide for themselves whether to take the examination.
D. Each of the employees have to decide for himself whether to take the examination.

25. A. The reason a new schedule is being prepared is that there has been a change in priorities. 25.____
B. Because there has been a change in priorities is the reason why a new schedule is being made up.
C. The reason why a new schedule is being made up is because there has been a change in priorities.
D. Because of a change in priorities is the reason why a new schedule is being prepared.

26. A. The changes in procedure had an unfavorable affect upon the output of the unit. 26.____
B. The increased output of the unit was largely due to the affect of the procedural changes.
C. The changes in procedure had the effect of increasing the output of the unit.
D. The increased output of the unit from the procedural changes were the effect.

Questions 27-33.

DIRECTIONS: Questions 27 through 33 are to be answered SOLELY on the basis of the information in the following extract, which is from a report prepared for Department X, which outlines the procedure to be followed in the case of transfers of employees.

Every transfer, regardless of the reason therefor, requires completion of the record of transfer, Form DT 411. To denote consent to the transfer, DT 411 should contain the signatures of the transferee and the personnel officer(s) concerned, except that, in the case of an involuntary transfer, the signatures of the transferee's present and prospective supervisors shall be entered in Boxes 8A and 8B, respectively, since the transferee does not consent. Only a permanent employee may request a transfer; in such cases, the employee's attendance record shall be duly considered with regard to absences, latenesses, and accrued overtime balances. In the case of an inter-district transfer, the employee's attendance record must be included in Section 8A of the transfer request, Form DT 410, by the personnel officer of the district from which the transfer is requested. The personnel officer of the district to which the employee requested transfer may refuse to accept accrued overtime balances in excess of ten days.

An employee on probation shall be eligible for transfer. If such employee is involuntarily transferred, he shall be credited for the period of time already served on probation. However, if such transfer is voluntary, the employee shall be required to serve the entire period of his probation in the new position. An employee who has occurred a disability which prevents him from performing his normal duties may be transferred during the period of such disability to other appropriate duties. A disability transfer requires the completion of either Form DT414 if the disability is job-connected, or Form DT 415 if it is not a job-connected disability. In either case, the personnel officer of the district from which the transfer is made signs in Box 6A of the first two copies and the personnel officer of the district to which the transfer is made signs in Box 6B of the last two copies; or, in the case of an intra-district disability transfer, the personnel officer must sign in Box 6A of the first two copies and Box 6B of the last two copies

27. When a personnel officer consents to an employee's request for transfer from his district, this procedure requires that the personnel officer sign Form(s) 27.____

    A. DT 411
    B. DT 410 and DT 411
    C. DT 411 and either Form DT 414 or DT 415
    D. DT 410 and DT 411, and either Form DT 414 or DT 415

28. With respect to the time record of an employee transferred against his wishes during his probationary period, this procedure requires that 28.____

    A. he serve the entire period of his probation in his present office
    B. he lose his accrued overtime balance
    C. his attendance record be considered with regard to absences and latenesses
    D. he be given credit for the period of time he has already served on probation

29. Assume you are a supervisor and an employee must be transferred into your office against his wishes. 29.____
    According to this procedure, the box you must sign on the record of transfer is

    A. 6A B. 8A C. 6B D. 8B

30. Under this procedure, in the case of a disability transfer, when must Box 6A on Forms DT 414 and DT 415 be signed by the personnel officer of the district to which the transfer is being made? 30.____

    A. In all cases when either Form DT 414 or Form DT 415 is used
    B. In all cases when Form DT 414 is used and only under certain circumstances when Form DT 415 is used
    C. In all cases when Form DT 415 is used and only under certain circumstances when Form DT 414 is used
    D. Only under certain circumstances when either Form DT 414 or Form DT 415 is used

31. From the above passage, it may be inferred MOST correctly that the number of copies of Form DT 414 is 31.____

    A. no more than 2
    B. at least 3
    C. at least 5
    D. more than the number of copies of Form DT 415

32. A change in punctuation and capitalization only which would change one sentence into two and possibly contribute to somewhat greater ease of reading of this report extract would be MOST appropriate in the _______ sentence, _______ paragraph. 32.____

A. 2nd; 1st
B. 3rd; 1st
C. next to the last; 2nd
D. 2nd; 2nd

33. In the second paragraph, a word that is INCORRECTLY used is _______ in the _______ sentence. 33.____

A. *shall;* 1st
B. *voluntary;* 3rd
C. *occurred;* 4th
D. *intra-district;* last

Questions 34-38.

DIRECTIONS: Questions 34 through 38 are to be answered SOLELY on the basis of the information contained in the following passage.

Positive discipline minimizes the amount of personal supervision required and aids in the maintenance of standards. When a new employee has been properly introduced and carefully instructed, when he has come to know the supervisor and has confidence in the supervisor's ability to take care of him, when he willingly cooperates with the supervisor, that employee has been under positive discipline and can be put on his own to produce the quantity and quality of work desired. Negative discipline, the fear of transfer to a less desirable location, for example, to a limited extent may restrain certain individuals from overt violation of rules and regulations governing attendance and conduct which in governmental agencies are usually on at least an agency-wide basis. Negative discipline may prompt employees to perform according to certain rules to avoid a penalty such as, for example, docking for tardiness.

34. According to the above passage, it is reasonable to assume that in the area of discipline, the first-line supervisor in a governmental agency has GREATER scope for action in 34.____

A. *positive* discipline because negative discipline is largely taken care of by agency rules and regulations
B. *negative* discipline because rules and procedures are already fixed and the supervisor can rely on them
C. *positive* discipline because the supervisor is in a position to recommend transfers
D. *negative* discipline because positive discipline is reserved for people on a higher supervisory level

35. In order to maintain positive discipline of employees under his supervision, it is MOST important for a supervisor to 35.____

A. assure each employee that he has nothing to worry about
B. insist at the outset on complete cooperation from employees
C. be sure that each employee is well trained in his job
D. inform new employees of the penalties for not meeting standards

36. According to the above passage, a feature of negative discipline is that it 36.____

A. may lower employee morale
B. may restrain employees from disobeying the rules
C. censures equal treatment of employees
D. tends to create standards for quality of work

37. A REASONABLE conclusion based on the above passage is that positive discipline benefits a supervisor because 37.____

A. he can turn over orientation and supervision of a new employee to one of his subordinates
B. subordinates learn to cooperate with one another when working on an assignment
C. it is easier to administer
D. it cuts down, in the long run, on the amount of time the supervisor needs to spend on direct supervision

38. Based on the above passage, it is REASONABLE to assume that an important difference between positive discipline and negative discipline is that positive discipline 38.____

A. is concerned with the quality of work and negative discipline with the quantity of work
B. leads to a more desirable basis for motivation of the employee
C. is more likely to be concerned with agency rules and regulations
D. uses fear while negative discipline uses penalties to prod employees to adequate performance

Questions 39-50.

DIRECTIONS: Questions 39 through 50 are to be answered on the basis of the information given in the graph and chart below.

8 (#2)

ENROLLMENT IN POSTGRADUATE STUDIES

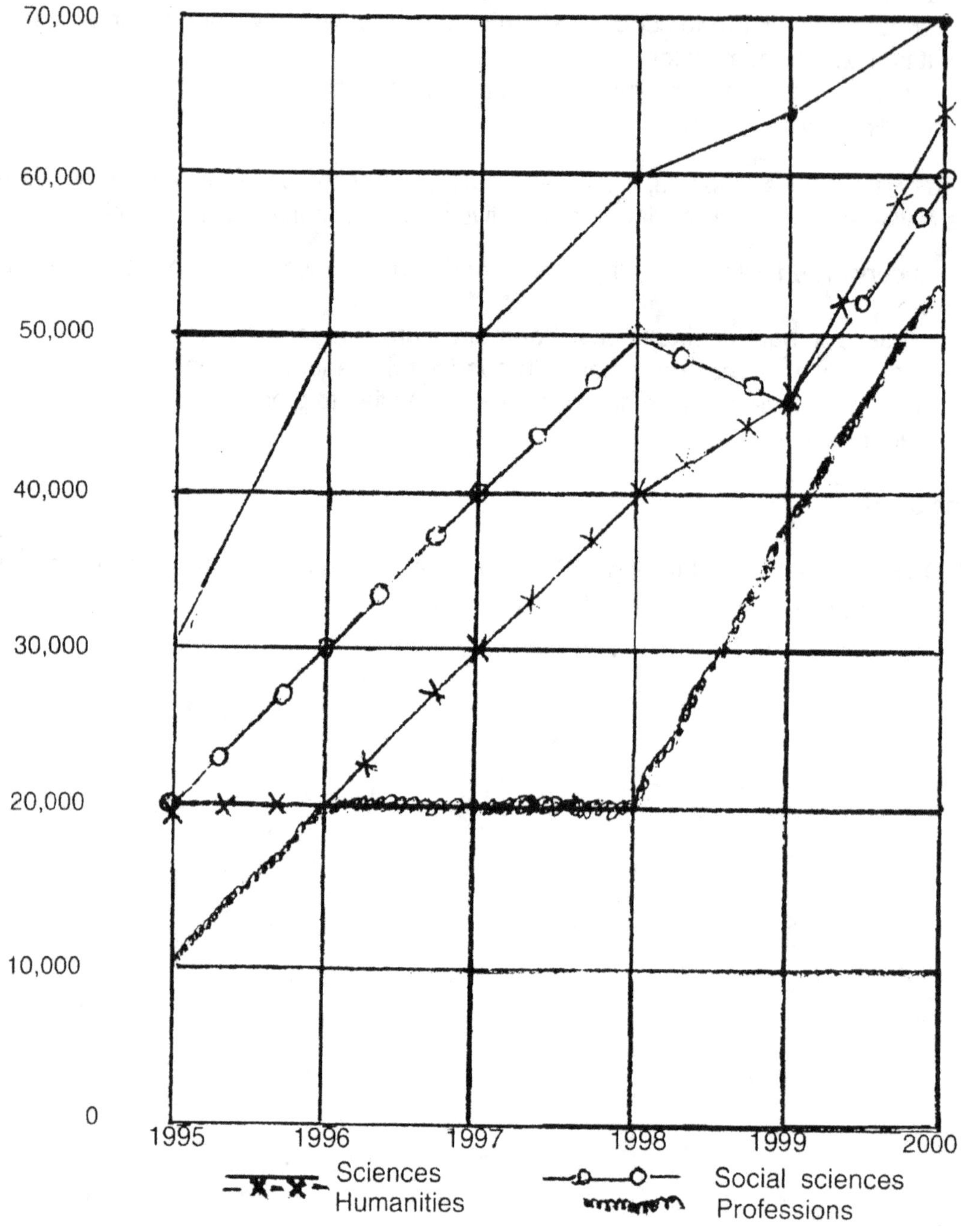

ENROLLMENT IN POSTGRADUATE STUDIES

Fields	Subdivisions	1999	2000
Sciences	Math	10,000	12,000
	Physical science	22,000	24,000
	Behavioral science	32,000	35,000
Humanities	Literature	26,000	34,000
	Philosophy	6,000	8,000
	Religion	4,000	6,000
	Arts	10,000	16,000
Social sciences	History	36,000	46,000
	Sociology	8,000	14.000
Professions	Law	2,000	2,000
	Medicine	6,000	8,000
	Business	30,000	44,000

39. The number of students enrolled in the social sciences and in the humanities was the same in _______ and _______. 39._____

A. 1997; 1999
B. 1995; 1999
C. 1999; 2000
D. 1996; 1999

40. A comparison of the enrollment of students in the various postgraduate studies shows that in every year from 1995 through 2000, there were more students enrolled in the _______ than in the _______. 40._____

A. professions; sciences
B. humanities; professions
C. social sciences; professions
D. humanities; sciences

41. The number of students enrolled in the humanities was GREATER than the number of students enrolled in the professions by the same amount in _______ of the years. 41._____

A. two
B. three
C. four
D. five

42. The one field of postgraduate study to show a decrease in enrollment in one year compared to the year immediately preceding is 42._____

A. humanities
B. sciences
C. professions
D. social sciences

43. If the proportion of arts students to all humanities students was the same in 1997 as in 2000, then the number of arts students in 1997 was 43._____

A. 7,500
B. 13,000
C. 15,000
D. 5,000

44. In which field of postgraduate study did enrollment INCREASE by 20 percent from 1997 to 1998? 44._____

A. Humanities
B. Professions
C. Sciences
D. Social sciences

45. The GREATEST increase in overall enrollment took place between 45._____

A. 1995 and 1996
B. 1997 and 1998
C. 1998 and 1999
D. 1999 and 2000

46. Between 1997 and 2000, the combined enrollment of the sciences and social sciences increased by 46.____

A. 40,000 B. 48,000 C. 50,000 D. 54,000

47. If the enrollment in the social sciences had decreased from 1999 to 2000 at the same rate as from 1998 to 1999, then the social science enrollment in 2000 would have differed from the humanities enrollment in 2000 *MOST* NEARLY by 47.____

A. 6,000 B. 8,000 C. 12,000 D. 22,000

48. In the humanities, the GREATEST percentage increase in enrollment from 1999 to 2000 was in 48.____

A. literature
B. philosophy
C. religion
D. arts

49. If the proportion of behavioral science students to the total number of students in the sciences was the same in 1996 as in 1999, then the increase in behavioral science enrollment from 1996 to 2000 was 49.____

A. 5,000 B. 7,000 C. 10,000 D. 14,000

50. If enrollment in the professions increased at the same rate from 2000 to 2001 as from 1999 to 2000, the enrollment in the professions in 2001 would be MOST NEARLY 50.____

A. 85,000 B. 75,000 C. 60,000 D. 55,000

KEY (CORRECT ANSWERS)

1. C	11. D	21. C	31. B	41. B
2. A	12. C	22. C	32. B	42. D
3. C	13. B	23. D	33. C	43. A
4. C	14. D	24. B	34. A	44. C
5. B	15. A	25. A	35. C	45. D
6. B	16. D	26. C	36. B	46. A
7. B	17. B	27. A	37. D	47. D
8. C	18. A	28. D	38. B	48. D
9. D	19. C	29. D	39. B	49. C
10. B	20. D	30. D	40. C	50. B

EXAMINATION SECTION
TEST 1

DIRECTIONS: Each question or incomplete statement is followed by several suggested answers or completions. Select the one that BEST answers the question or completes the statement. *PRINT THE LETTER OF THE CORRECT ANSWER IN THE SPACE AT THE RIGHT.*

1. You have recently been assigned to a new office and are expected to supervise six clerks. 1._____
All of the following would be good introductory steps to take EXCEPT

   A. giving a clear presentation of yourself to the clerks, including a short summary of your recent work experience
   B. initiating informal discussions with each clerk concerning his work
   C. making a general survey of all the functions which each clerk has been performing
   D. making a list of the duties each clerk is required to perform and giving it to the clerk

2. Your supervisor has advised you that a specific aspect of a job is being done incorrectly and you acknowledge the mistake. 2._____
Of the following, the MOST efficient way of dealing with this situation is to

   A. call a meeting of the clerks who are performing this particular function and explain the correct method
   B. assume the blame and correct the errors as they are given to you
   C. speak with each clerk individually and carefully show each one the proper method
   D. distribute a set of written instructions covering all clerical procedures to the employees doing that particular job

3. A new department regulation calls for a change in a particular method of processing new applications. Two clerks have complained to you that the new method is more time-consuming, and they prefer to do it the original way. 3._____
Of the following, what is the MOST advisable thing to do?

   A. Discuss the situation with them and attempt to determine whether they are utilizing the method properly.
   B. Discuss the advantages of both methods with them and let them use the one that is more practical.
   C. Firmly instruct the clerks to proceed with the new method since it is not up to them to refute department policy.
   D. Tell them to survey the opinions of the other clerks on this matter and inform you of the results.

4. A member of the clerical staff has recently begun reporting late for work rather regularly. On each occasion, the individual presented an excuse, but the latenesses continue. 4._____
Of the following, the MOST advisable action for her supervisor to take is to

   A. have a staff meeting and stress the importance of being on time for work, without singling out the specific individual
   B. put a notice on the departmental office bulletin board, specifying and stressing that lateness can not be tolerated

C. talk privately with the individual to determine whether theré are any unusual circumstances that might be causing the lateness
D. send the individual a memorandum clearly indicating that continual lateness will result in disciplinary action

5. Assume that, as the supervisor of a unit, you have been asked to prepare a vacation schedule for your subordinate employees. The employees have had different lengths of service. Some of them have already submitted requests for certain weeks. 5._____
Of the following, which factor would be LEAST important in setting up this schedule?

A. Your opinion of each employee's past work performance
B. Each employee's preference for a vacation period
C. The amount of work the unit is expected to accomplish during the vacation period
D. The number of employees who have requested to go on vacation at the same time

6. Your superior finds that he must leave the office one day before he has had time to check and sign the day's correspondence. He asks you to proofread the letters, have corrections made where necessary, and then sign his name. You have never signed his name before. 6._____
Of the following, the BEST thing for you to do is to

A. sign your superior's name in full, making it look as much like his handwriting as possible
B. sign your superior's name and your own name in full as proof that you signed for him
C. sign your superior's name in full and add your initials to show that the signature is not his own
D. politely refuse to sign his name because it is forgery

7. The head of your office sometimes makes handwritten notations on original letters which he receives and requests that you mail the letters back to the sender. Of the following, the BEST action for you to take FIRST is to 7._____

A. request that this practice be stopped because it does not provide for a record in the files
B. request that this practice be stopped because it is not the customary way to respond to letters
C. photocopy the letters so that there are copies for the file and then send the letters out
D. ask the head of your office if he wants you to keep any record of the letters

8. The main function of most agency administrative offices is *information management.* Information that is received by an administrative office may be classified as active (information which requires the recipient to take some action) or passive (information which does not require action). 8._____
Which one of the following items received must clearly be treated as ACTIVE information?
A(n)

A. confirmation of payment
B. press release concerning an agency event
C. advertisement for a new restaurant opening near the agency
D. request for a student transcript

9. Which of the following statements about the use of the photocopy process is CORRECT? 9.____

   A. It is difficult to use.
   B. It can be used to reproduce color.
   C. It does not print well on colored paper.
   D. Once source documents have been used, they cannot be used again.

10. In order to get the BEST estimate of how long a repetitive office procedure should take, a supervisor should find out how 10.____

   A. long it takes her best worker to do the procedure once on a typical day
   B. long it takes her best and worst workers to do the procedure once on a typical day
   C. much time her best worker spends on the procedure during a typical week and the total number of times the worker executes the procedure during the same week
   D. much time all her subordinates spend on the procedure during a typical week and the total number of times the procedure was executed during the same week by all employees

11. Of the following, the MOST suitable and appropriate way to make 250 copies of a particular form is to 11.____

   A. print all 250 copies on the office computer
   B. delegate the work to someone else
   C. reproduce it on a photocopying machine
   D. use an offset printing process

Questions 12-18.

DIRECTIONS: Questions 12 through 18 are to be answered on the basis of the extracts shown below from Federal withholding tables. These tables indicate the amounts which must be withheld from the employee's salary by his employer for Federal income tax and for social security. They are based on weekly earnings.

INCOME TAX WITHHOLDING TABLE

The wages are -		And the number of withholding exemptions claimed is-					
At least	But less than	0	1	2	3	4	5
		The amount of income tax to be withheld shall be -					
$200	$205	$14.10	$11.80	$ 9.50	$ 7.20	$ 4.90	$2.80
205	210	14.90	12.60	10.30	8.00	5.70	3.50
210	215	15.70	13.40	11.10	8.80	6.50	4.20
215	220	16.50	14.20	11.90	9.60	7.30	5.00
220	225	17.30	15.00	12.70	10.40	8.10	5.80
225	230	18.10	15.80	13.50	11.20	8.90	6.60
230	235	18.90	16.60	14.30	12.00	9.70	7.40
235	240	19.70	17.40	15.10	12.80	10.50	8.20
240	245	20.50	18.20	15.90	13.60	11.30	9.00
245	250	21.30	19.00	16.70	14.40	12.10	9.80

SOCIAL SECURITY EMPLOYEE TAX TABLE

Wages		Tax to be withheld	Wages		Tax to be withheld
At least	But less than		At least	But less than	
$202.79	$202.99	$15.35	$229.72	$229.91	$16.75
202.99	203.18	15.36	229.91	230.10	16.76
203.18	203.37	15.37	230.10	230.29	16.77
203.37	203.56	15.38	230.29	230.49	16.78
203.56	203.75	15.39	230.49	230.68	16.79
203.75	203.95	15.40	230.68	230.87	16.80
203.95	204.14	15.41	230.87	231.06	16.81
204.14	204.33	15.42	231.06	231.25	16.82
204.33	204.52	15.43	231.25	231.45	16.83
204.52	204.72	15.44	231.45	231.64	16.84

Wages		Tax to be withheld	Wages		Tax to be withheld
At least	But less than		At least	But less than	
$222.02	$222.22	$16.35	$234.52	$234.72	$17.00
222.22	222.41	16.36	234.72	234.91	17.01
222.41	222.60	16.37	234.91	235.10	17.02
222.60	222.79	16.38	235.10	235.29	17.03
222.79	222.99	16.39	235.29	235.49	17.04
222.99	223.18	16.40	235.49	235.68	17.05
223.18	223.37	16.41	235.68	235.87	17.06
223.37	223.56	16.42	235.87	236.06	17.07
223.56	223.75	16.43	236.06	236.25	17.08
223.75	223.95	16.44	236.25	236.45	17.09

12. Dave Andes has wages of $242.75 for one week. He has claimed three withholding exemptions. 12.____
What is the Federal income tax which should be withheld?

A. $13.60 B. $15.90 C. $18.20 D. $20.50

13. Mary Hodes has wages of $229.95 for one week. 13.____
What is the Social Security tax which should be withheld?

A. $16.75 B. $16.76 C. $16.77 D. $16.78

14. Joe Jones had wages of $235.63 for one week. He has claimed two withholding exemptions. 14.____
What is the Federal income tax which should be withheld?

A. $12.80 B. $14.30 C. $15.10 D. $17.40

15. Tom Stein had wages of $203.95 for one week. What is the Social Security tax which should be withheld? 15.____

A. $15.40 B. $15.41 C. $16.05 D. $16.06

16. Robert Helman had wages of $222.80 for one week. He has claimed one withholding exemption. 16.____
If only Federal income tax and Social Security tax were deducted from his earnings for the same week, how much *take-home* pay should he have for the week?

A. $191.41 B. $193.96 C. $194.12 D. $195.65

17. Audrey Stein has wages of $203.00 for one week. She claimed no withholding exemptions. 17.____
If only Federal income tax and Social Security tax were deducted from her earnings for the same week, how much *take-home* pay should she have for the week?

A. $171.84 B. $172.34 C. $173.54 D. $175.84

18. Anthony Covallo, who worked 28 hours in the past week, has a regular hourly rate of $7.25 per hour and earns a premium of time and a half for hours over 40. He has claimed four withholding exemptions. 18.____
After Social Security tax and Federal income tax are deducted from his wages for the past week, how much pay does he have left?

A. $180.98 B. $181.13 C. $182.29 D. $182.74

19. In judging the adequacy of a standard office form, which of the following is LEAST important? 19.____
_______ of the form.

A. Date B. Legibility C. Size D. Design

20. Clear and accurate telephone messages should be taken for employees who are out of the office. 20.____
Which of the following is of LEAST importance when taking a telephone message?

A. Name of the person called
B. Name of the caller

C. Details of the message
D. Time of the call

21. Suppose that all office supplies are kept in a centrally located cabinet in the office. Of the following, which is usually the BEST policy to adhere to for distribution of supplies? 21.____

A. Permit employees to stock up on all supplies to avoid frequent trips to the cabinet.
B. Assign one employee to be in charge of distributing all supplies to other employees at frequent intervals.
C. Inform employees that supplies should be taken in large quantities and only when needed.
D. Keep cabinet closed and instruct employees that they must check with you before taking supplies.

Questions 22-25.

DIRECTIONS: Questions 22 through 25 are to be answered SOLELY on the basis of the following passage.

Use of the systems and procedures approach to office management is revolutionizing the supervision of office work. This approach views an enterprise as an entity which seeks to fulfill definite objectives. Systems and procedures help to organize repetitive work into a routine, thus reducing the amount of decision-making required for its accomplishment. As a result, employees are guided in their efforts and perform only necessary work. Supervisors are relieved of any details of execution and are free to attend to more important work. Establishing work guides which require that identical tasks be performed the same way each, time permits standardization of forms, machine operations, work methods, and controls. This approach also reduces the probability of errors. Any error committed is usually discovered quickly because the incorrect work does not meet the requirement of the work guides. Errors are also reduced through work specialization which allows each employee to become thoroughly proficient in a particular type of work. Such proficiency also tends to improve the morale of the employees.

22. Of the following, which one BEST expresses the main theme of the above passage? The 22.____

A. advantages and disadvantages of the systems and procedures approach to office management
B. effectiveness of the systems and procedures approach to office management in developing skills
C. systems and procedures approach to office management as it relates to office costs
D. advantages of the systems and procedures approach to office management for supervisors and office workers

23. Work guides are LEAST likely to be used when 23.____

A. standardized forms are used
B. a particular office task is distinct and different from all others
C. identical tasks are to be performed in identical ways
D. similar work methods are expected from each employee

24. According to the above passage, when an employee makes a work error, it USUALLY 24.____

    A. is quickly corrected by the supervisor
    B. necessitates a change in the work guides
    C. can be detected quickly if work guides are in use
    D. increases the probability of further errors by that employee

25. The above passage states that the accuracy of an employee's work is INCREASED by 25.____

    A. using the work specialization approach
    B. employing a probability sample
    C. requiring him to shift at one time into different types of tasks
    D. having his supervisor check each detail of work execution

---

KEY (CORRECT ANSWERS)

1.	D	11.	C
2.	A	12.	A
3.	A	13.	B
4.	C	14.	C
5.	A	15.	B
6.	C	16.	A
7.	D	17.	C
8.	D	18.	D
9.	B	19.	A
10.	D	20.	D

21.	B
22.	D
23.	B
24.	C
25.	A

TEST 2

DIRECTIONS: Each question or incomplete statement is followed by several suggested answers or completions. Select the one that BEST answers the question or completes the statement. *PRINT THE LETTER OF THE CORRECT ANSWER IN THE SPACE AT THE RIGHT.*

1. A certain supervisor often holds group meetings with subordinates to discuss the goals of the unit and manpower requirements for meeting objectives. 1.____
   For the supervisor to hold such meetings is a

   A. *good* practice because it will aid both the supervisor and subordinates in planning and completing the unit's work
   B. *good* practice because it will prevent future problems from interfering with the unit's objectives
   C. *poor* practice because the supervisor has the sole responsibility for meeting objectives and should make manpower decisions without any advice
   D. *poor* practice because the subordinates will be allowed to set their own work quotas

2. Assume that you are a supervisor who has been asked to evaluate the work of a clerk who was transferred to your unit about six months ago. 2.____
   Which one of the following, by itself, provides the BEST basis for making such an evaluation?

   A. Ask the clerk's former supervisor about the employee's previous work.
   B. Ask the clerk's co-workers for their opinions of the employee's work.
   C. Evaluate the quantity and quality of the employee's work over the six-month period.
   D. Observe the employee's performance from time to time during the next week and base your evaluation on these observations.

3. Which of the following would be the MOST desirable way for a supervisor to help improve the job performance of a particular subordinate? 3.____

   A. Criticize the employee's performance in front of other employees.
   B. Privately warn the employee that failure to meet work standards may lead to dismissal.
   C. Hold a meeting with this employee and other subordinates in which the need to improve the unit's performance is stressed.
   D. Meet privately with the employee and discuss both positive and negative aspects of the employee's work

4. Suppose that your office has a limited supply of a pamphlet which people may read in your office when they seek certain information, but another office in your building is supposed to have a large supply available for distribution to the public. 4.____
   Which of the following would be the BEST thing for you to do when someone states that he has not been able to obtain one of these pamphlets?

   A. Tell him that he misunderstood the directions that other employees have given him and carefully direct him to the other office.
   B. Ask whether he has visited the other office and requested a copy from them.
   C. Let him take one of your office's copies of the pamphlet and then call the other office and ask why they have run out of copies for distribution.

D. Tell him that your office does its best to keep the public informed but that this might not be true of other offices.

5. On Monday, a clerk made many errors in completing a new daily record form. The supervisor explained the errors and had the clerk correct the form. On Tuesday, the clerk made fewer errors. Because he was very busy, the supervisor did not point out the errors to the clerk but corrected the errors himself. On Wednesday, the clerk made the same number of errors as on Tuesday. The supervisor reprimanded the clerk for making so many errors. 5.____
The supervisor's handling of this situation on Wednesday may be considered poor MAINLY because the

A. clerk was not given enough time to complete each form properly
B. supervisor should not have expected improvement without further training
C. clerk was obviously incapable of completing the form
D. supervisor should have continued to correct the errors himself

Questions 6-8.

DIRECTIONS: Questions 6 through 8 are to be answered SOLELY on the basis of the information contained in the following passage.

When using words like company, association, *council, committee, and board in place of the full official name, the writer should not capitalize these short forms unless he intends them to invoke the full force of the institution's authority. In legal contracts, in minutes, or in formal correspondence where one is speaking formally and officially on behalf of the company, the term "Company" is usually capitalized, but in ordinary usage, where it is not essential to load the short form with this significance, capitalization would be excessive. (Example: The company will have many good openings for graduates this June.)*

The treatment recommended for short forms of place names is essentially the same as that recommended for short forms of organizational names. In general, we capitalize the full form but not the short form. If Park Avenue is referred to in one sentence, then "the avenue" is sufficient in subsequent references. The same is true with words like building, hotel, station, and airport, which are capitalized when part of a proper name (Pan Am Building, Hotel Plaza, Union Station, O'Hare Airport) but are simply lower-cased when replacing these specific names.

6. The above passage states that USUALLY the short forms of names of organizations 6.____

A. and places should not be capitalized
B. and places should be capitalized
C. should not be capitalized, but the short forms of names of places should be capitalized
D. should be capitalized, but the short forms of names of places should not be capitalized

7. The above passage states that in legal contracts, in minutes, and in formal correspondence, the short forms of names of organizations should 7.____

A. usually not be capitalized
B. usually be capitalized
C. usually not be used
D. never be used

8. It can be INFERRED from the above passage that decisions regarding when to capitalize certain words 8.____

   A. should be left to the discretion of the writer
   B. should be based on generally accepted rules
   C. depend on the total number of words capitalized
   D. are of minor importance

9. The Central Terminal and the Gardens Terminal are located on Glover Street. 9.____
   In ordinary usage, if this sentence were to be followed by the sentence in the choices below, which form of the sentence would be CORRECT?

   A. Both Terminals are situated on the same street.
   B. Both terminals are situated on the same Street.
   C. Both terminals are situated on the same street.
   D. Both Terminals are situated on the same Street.

10. A stylus is a(n) 10.____

   A. implement for writing containing a cylinder of graphite
   B. implement for writing with ink or a similar fluid
   C. pointed implement used to write
   D. stick of colored wax used for writing

11. As a supervisor, you have the responsibility of teaching new employees the functions and procedures of your office after their orientation by the personnel office. 11.____
   Of the following, the BEST way to begin such instruction is to

   A. advise the new employee of the benefits and services available to him, over and above his salary
   B. discuss the negative aspects of the departmental procedures and indicate methods available to overcome them
   C. assist the new employee in understanding the general purpose of the office procedures and how they fit in with the overall operation
   D. give a detailed briefing of the operations of your office, its functions and procedures

12. Assume that you are the supervisor of a clerical unit. One of the duties of the employees in your unit is to conduct a brief interview with persons using the services of your agency for the first time. The purpose of the interview is to get general background information in order to best direct them to the appropriate division. 12.____
   A clerk comes to your office and says that a prospective client has just called her some rather unpleasant names, accused her of being nosey and meddlesome, and has stated emphatically that she refuses to talk with an *underling,* meaning the clerk. The young woman is almost in tears. Of the following, what is the FIRST action you should take?

   A. Immediately call the agency's protection officer, have him advise the client of the regulations, and tell her that she will be removed if she is not more polite.
   B. Calm the clerk, introduce yourself to the client, and quietly discuss the agency's services, regulations, and informational needs, and request that she complete the interview with the clerk.

C. Calm the clerk, have her return and firmly advise the client of the agency's rules concerning the need for this first interview.
D. Introduce yourself to the client and advise her that without an apology to the clerk and completion of the interview, she will not be given any service.

13. A recent high school graduate has just been assigned to the unit which you supervise. Which of the following would be the LEAST desirable technique to use with this employee? 13.____

A. At any one time, give the new employee only as much detail about the job as the employee can absorb.
B. Always tell the new employee the correct procedure, then demonstrate how it is accomplished.
C. Assign the employee the same quantity and type of work that the other employees are doing to see if the employee can handle the job.
D. Assume the employee is tense and be prepared to repeat procedures and descriptions.

14. Assume that you supervise a work unit of several employees. Which of the following is LEAST essential in assuring that the goals which you set for the unit are achieved? 14.____

A. Establishing objectives and standards for the staff
B. Providing justification for disciplinary action
C. Measuring performance or progress of individuals against standards
D. Taking corrective action where performance is less than expected

15. One of the clerks you supervise is often reluctant to accept assignments and usually complains about the amount of work expected, although the other clerks with the same assignments and workload seem quite happy. 15.____
Of the following, the MOST accurate assumption that you can make about this clerk is that she

A. will require additional observation and help
B. will eventually have to be discharged or transferred
C. is incompetent
D. is overworked

Questions 16-21.

DIRECTIONS: Questions 16 through 21 are to be answered SOLELY on the basis of the airline timetable and the information appearing on the last page of this test.

Fact Situation:

An administrator wants you to purchase airline tickets for him so that he can attend a meeting being held in Chicago on Monday. He must leave from LaGuardia Airport in New York on Monday morning as late as possible but with arrival in Chicago no later than 9:00 A.M. He wishes to fly coach/economy class both ways. The meeting is due to end at 5:30 P.M., and he wishes to obtain the first plane after 6:45 P.M. going back to LaGuardia Airport. If all these requirements have been met, he would, if possible, also like to fly to and leave from Midway Airport in Chicago and go non-stop both ways.

16. You should obtain a ticket for the administrator from New York to Chicago on flight number 16.____

A. 483 B. 201 C. 277 D. 539

17. You should obtain a ticket for the administrator from Chicago to New York on flight number 17.____

A. 588 B. 692 C. 268 D. 334

18. The administrator decides to take limousines to and from both airports. 18.____
If the limousine charge in Chicago is $52.50. and there is no reduced rate for a round-trip flight, what is the cost of the administrator's round-trip air fare PLUS limousine service?

A. $827.50 B. $931.00 C. $963.00 D. $967.00

19. The administrator asked you whether he would be able to get breakfast on his flight to Chicago or whether he should go to the airport early and eat there before boarding the plane. He prefers to eat on the plane. 19.____
Of the following, the BEST reply to make is:

A. I will have to telephone the airport to find out
B. You should eat at the airport
C. A meal is served on the plane
D. Only certain passengers get a meal on the plane

20. Of the following requests of the administrator concerning his travel arrangements, which one is IMPOSSIBLE to meet? 20.____

A. Chicago arrival no later than 9 A.M.
B. New York departure from LaGuardia Airport
C. Non-stop flights both ways
D. Chicago departure from Midway Airport

21. Suppose that it is necessary to take a first-class seat on the trip to Chicago although you have no problem reserving a coach/economy seat on the return trip. 21.____
If there is no reduction in fare for round-trip flights, how much MORE will this trip cost than round-trip coach/ economy?

A. $209 B. $236 C. $318 D. $636

22. Ms. X, a clerk under your supervision, has been working in the unit for a few weeks. Some of the other employees have complained to you that Ms. X has an annoying habit of constantly tapping her feet on the floor and it disturbs their work. 22.____
The BEST thing for you to do is to

A. ignore the complaints because the employees should be concerned only with their own habits
B. speak with Ms. X privately and discuss the situation with her
C. make a general announcement that employees should control their nervous habits
D. observe Ms. X for a few weeks to see if the employees are correct, and then take action

23. Suppose you answer a telephone call from someone who states that he is a friend of one of your co-workers and needs the employee's new address in order to send an invitation. Your co-worker is on vacation but you know her address. Which of the following is the BEST action for you to take? 23.____

A. Give the caller the address but ask the caller not to mention that you are the one who gave it out.
B. Give the caller the address and leave a note for your co-worker stating what you did.
C. Tell the caller you do not know the address but will give the employee's phone number if that will help.
D. Offer to take his name and address and have your co-worker contact him.

24. Assume that you receive a telephone call in which the caller requests information which you know is posted in the office next to yours. You start to tell the caller you will transfer her call to the right office, but she interrupts you and says she has been transferred from office to office and is tired of getting a *run-around*. Of the following, the BEST thing for you to do is to 24.____

A. give the caller the phone number of the office next to yours and quickly end the conversation
B. give her the phone number of the office next to yours and tell her you will try to transfer her call
C. ask her if she wants to hold on while you get the information for her
D. tell the caller that she could have avoided the *run-around* by asking for the right office, and suggest that she come in person

25. Assume that your unit processes confidential forms which are submitted by persons seeking financial assistance. An individual comes to your office, gives you his name, and states that he would like to look over a form which he sent in about a week ago because he believes he omitted some important information. Of the following, the BEST thing for you to do FIRST is to 25.____

A. locate the proper form
B. call the individual's home telephone number to verify his identity
C. ask the individual if he has proof of his identity
D. call the security office

KEY (CORRECT ANSWERS)

1. A
2. C
3. D
4. B
5. B
6. A
7. B
8. B
9. C
10. C
11. C
12. B
13. C
14. B
15. A
16. A
17. D
18. B
19. C
20. D
21. C
22. B
23. D
24. C
25. C

EXAMINATION SECTION
TEST 1

DIRECTIONS: Each question or incomplete statement is followed by several suggested answers or completions. Select the one that BEST answers the question or completes the statement. *PRINT THE LETTER OF THE CORRECT ANSWER IN THE SPACE AT THE RIGHT.*

1. Assume that your supervisor has placed you in complete charge of an important project and that several clerks have been assigned to assist you. You have been given authority to establish any new procedures or revise existing procedures in order to complete the project as soon as possible. Just before you begin work on the project, one of the clerks suggests a change in the procedure which you realize at once would result in completion of the project in about half the time you expected to spend on it. 1.____
Of the following, the MOST effective course of action for you to take is to

   A. adopt the suggestion immediately to expedite the completion of the project
   B. discuss the suggestion with your superior to obtain his consent to the change
   C. point out to the clerk that an adequate procedure has already been established, but that his suggestion may be used in future projects of this type
   D. encourage the other clerks to make further suggestions

2. A supervisor of a unit may safely delegate certain of his functions to his subordinates. 2.____
Of the following, the function which can MOST safely be delegated is the

   A. settlement of employee grievances
   B. planning and scheduling of the production of the unit
   C. improvement of production methods of the unit
   D. maintenance of records of the work output of the unit

3. Some organizations now question the effectiveness of extreme job specialization. It is felt that in some instances, it may be more advantageous to enlarge the scope of individual jobs, thus providing the employee with a greater variety of tasks. 3.____
Of the following, the one which is LEAST likely to be a result of enlarging the scope of jobs is a(n)

   A. increase in the employee's job responsibilities
   B. decrease in the number of job titles in the organization
   C. increase in the number of tasks performed by an employee
   D. decrease in employee flexibility

4. A manual that is essentially designed to present detailed procedures and policies is not necessarily a good training medium, nor is a manual designed for high-level administrators likely to be satisfactory for use at lower levels. The MOST valid implication of this statement is that 4.____

   A. a manual to be effective should be flexible enough to apply to any working level in an organization
   B. the uses to which a manual will be put and the people who will use it should be carefully determined before it is prepared
   C. the more detailed procedures a manual contains, the more effective it will be for the use of administrators

D. the degree of difficulty encountered in the preparation of a manual varies with the purpose for which it is designed and the people for whom it is written

5. In assigning a complicated task to a group of subordinates, Mr. Jones, a unit supervisor, neither indicates the specific steps to be followed in performing the assignment nor designates the subordinate to be responsible for seeing that the task is done on time. This supervisor's method of assigning the task is MOST likely to result in 5.____

A. the loss of skills previously acquired by his subordinates
B. assumption of authority by the most capable subordinates
C. friction and misunderstanding among subordinates with consequent delays in work
D. greater individual effort and self-reliance on the part of his subordinates

6. Assume that the head of your agency has appointed you to a committee that has been assigned the task of reviewing the clerical procedures used in a large bureau of the agency and of recommending appropriate changes in the procedures where necessary. Of the following, the FIRST step that should be taken by the committee in carrying out its assignment is to 6.____

A. survey the most efficient procedures used in comparable agencies
B. study the organization of the bureau and the work it is required to do
C. evaluate the possible effects of proposed revisions in the procedures
D. determine the effectiveness of existing procedures

7. A recently developed practice in administration favors reducing the number of levels of authority in an organization, increasing the number of subordinates reporting to a superior, and also increasing the authority delegated to the subordinates. This practice would MOST likely result in a(n) 7.____

A. increase in the span of control exercised by superiors
B. increase in detailed information that flows to a superior from each subordinate
C. decrease in the responsibility exercised by the subordinates
D. decrease in the number of functions performed by the organization

8. As an organization grows larger, the amount of personal contact between the top administrative officials and the rank and file employees diminishes. Consequently, management comes to rely more heavily upon written reports and records for securing information and exercising control. The MOST valid implication of this statement is that, as an organization grows larger, 8.____

A. evaluation of the work of rank and file employees becomes more objective because of greater reliance upon written reports and records
B. relations between first line supervisors and their subordinates grow more impersonal
C. top administrative officials depend upon less direct methods for controlling the work of their subordinates
D. it becomes more difficult for top administrative officials to maintain high morale among rank and file employees

9. A supervisor whose unit has a good production record is usually found to be more occupied with the functions associated with leadership than with the performance of the same functions as his subordinates. The MOST valid implication of this statement is that 9.____

A. a supervisor whose unit has a good production record usually is not as competent in performing routine tasks as are his subordinates
B. ability to lead and competence in performing the day-to-day tasks of his subordinates are the requirements of a successful supervisor
C. a supervisor who spends more time on planning and organizing the work of his unit than on performing the routine tasks of his subordinates will find that his unit's production record will be good
D. a supervisor whose unit has a good production record usually places less emphasis on performing the day-to-day tasks of his subordinates than on planning the work of his unit

10. To delegate work is one of the main functions of the supervisor. In delegating work, the supervisor should remember that even though an assignment is delegated to a subordinate, the supervisor ultimately is responsible for seeing that the work is done. The MOST valid implication of this statement for a supervisor is that he should 10.____

A. delegate as few difficult tasks as possible so as to minimize the consequences of inadequate performance by his subordinates
B. delegate to his subordinates those tasks which he considers difficult or time-consuming
C. check the progress of delegated assignments periodically to make certain that the work is being done properly
D. assign work to a subordinate without holding him directly accountable for carrying it out

11. A unit supervisor should select and develop an understudy to take charge of the unit in the supervisor's absence and to assist the supervisor whenever necessary. Of the following, the technique that would be LEAST effective in developing an understudy is for the supervisor to 11.____

A. permit him to exercise complete supervision over certain parts of the work
B. assign him to work in which there is little likelihood of his making mistakes, so as to increase his self-confidence
C. accustom him to making reports on the progress of work he is supervising
D. give him responsibility gradually so that he will have time to absorb each new responsibility

12. A procedure manual of a public agency is potentially more usable than are files of individual messages or bulletins, but usability and usefulness are not routine by-products of the manual form. The MOST valid implication of this is that 12.____

A. the purpose of a manual should not be confined to an explanation of routine procedures
B. a manual may prove to be unsuitable for some of its anticipated uses
C. individual messages or bulletins are more likely to be of use than are manuals
D. a manual suffers from certain limitations that are not found in individual messages or bulletins

13. As the supervisor of a unit in a city agency, you have just been instructed to put into effect a new procedure which you know will be disliked by your subordinates. Of the following, the MOST important reason for calling a meeting of your staff before putting the new procedure into effect is to 13.____

    A. help you to determine which workers will be reluctant to cooperate in carrying out the new procedure
    B. allow you to announce that the new procedure must be put into effect despite any objections which might be raised
    C. enable you to explain that you don't approve of the new procedure and to give the reasons why it must nevertheless be put into effect
    D. permit you to discuss the purpose of the new procedure and to present the reasons for its adoption

14. Assume that you are a training conference leader and that you have just begun a series of conferences on supervisory techniques for new supervisors. Each conference is scheduled to last for three hours. A thorough discussion of all the material planned for the first session, which you had estimated would last until 4 P.M., is completed by 3:30 P.M. 14.____
    For you to summarize the points that have been made and close the meeting would be

    A. *advisable;* the participants will lose interest in the conference if it is permitted to continue merely to occupy the remaining time
    B. *inadvisable;* the participants should be asked if there are any other topics that they would like to discuss
    C. *advisable;* the participants in a training conference should not be kept from their regular work for long periods of time
    D. *inadvisable;* material scheduled for discussion at future sessions should be used for the remainder of this session

15. In any public agency, the top administrative officials are concerned largely with the work of overall creative planning with respect to the anticipated progress of the agency. The first-line supervisors, on the other hand, are concerned largely with the control of current action for the execution of current jobs. 15.____
    On the basis of this statement, a first-line supervisor would be CHIEFLY responsible for

    A. increasing or decreasing the responsibilities of his unit to reflect changes in the policies of the agency
    B. modifying the work assignments of his present staff to handle a seasonal variation in the activities of the unit
    C. revising the procedure that is used for transmitting instructions from the head of the agency to the unit heads
    D. raising and lowering the production goals of his unit as often as necessary to adjust them to the abilities of his subordinates

16. The control of clerical work in a public agency appears impossible if the clerical work is regarded merely as a series of duties unrelated to the functions of the agency. However, this control becomes feasible when it is realized that clerical work links and coordinates the functions of the agency. 16.____
    On the basis of this statement, the MOST accurate of the following statements is that the

A. complexity of clerical work may not be fully understood by those assigned to control it
B. clerical work can be readily controlled if it is coordinated by other work of the agency
C. number of clerical tasks may be reduced by regarding coordination as the function of clerical work
D. purposes of clerical work must be understood to make possible its proper control

17. Assume that as supervisor of a unit, you are to prepare a vacation schedule for the employees in your unit. Of the following, the factor which is LEAST important for you to consider in setting up this schedule is 17.____

A. the vacation preferences of each employee in the unit
B. the anticipated work load in the unit during the vacation period
C. how well each employee has performed his work
D. how essential a specific employee's services will be during the vacation period

18. In order to promote efficiency and economy in an agency, it is advisable for the management of systematize and standardize procedures and relationships insofar as this can be done; however, excessive routinizing which does not permit individual contributions or achievements should be avoided. 18.____
On the basis of this statement, it is MOST accurate to state that

A. systematized procedures should be designed mainly to encourage individual achievements
B. standardized procedures should allow for individual accomplishments
C. systematization of procedures may not be possible in organizations which have a large variety of functions
D. individual employees of an organization must fully accept standardized procedures if the procedures are to be effective

19. Trained employees work most efficiently and with a minimum expenditure of time and energy. Suitable equipment and definite, well-developed procedures are effective only when employees know how to use the equipment and procedures. 19.____
This statement means MOST NEARLY that

A. employees can be trained most efficiently when suitable equipment and definite procedures are used
B. training of employees is a costly but worthwhile investment
C. suitable equipment and definite procedures are of greatest value when employees have been properly trained to use them
D. the cost of suitable equipment and definite procedures is negligible when the saving in time and energy that they bring is considered

20. Assume that your supervisor has asked you to present to him comprehensive, periodic reports on the progress that your unit is making in meeting its work goals. 20.____
For you to give your superior oral reports rather than written ones is

A. *desirable;* it will be easier for him to transmit your oral reports to his superiors
B. *undesirable;* the oral reports will provide no permanent record to which he may refer
C. *undesirable;* there will be less opportunity for you to discuss the oral reports with him than the written ones

D. *desirable;* the oral reports will require little time and effort to prepare

21. Assume that an employee under your supervision complains to you that your evaluation of his work is too low. 21.____
The MOST appropriate action for you to take first is to

A. explain how you arrived at the evaluation of his work
B. encourage him to improve the quality of his work by pointing out specifically how he can do so
C. suggest that he appeal to an impartial higher authority if he disagrees with your evaluation
D. point out to him specific instances in which his work has been unsatisfactory

22. The nature of the experience and education that are made a prerequisite to employment determines in large degree the training job to be done after employment begins. 22.____
On the basis of this statement, it is MOST accurate to state that

A. the more comprehensive the experience and education required for employment, the more extensive the training that is usually given after appointment
B. the training that is given to employees depends upon the experience and education required of them before appointment
C. employees who possess the experience and education required for employment should need little additional training after appointment
D. the nature of the work that employees are expected to perform determines the training that they will need

23. Assume that you are preparing a report evaluating the work of a clerk who was transferred to your unit from another unit in the agency about a year ago. 23.____
Of the following, the method that would probably be MOST helpful to you in making this evaluation is to

A. consult the evaluations this employee received from his former supervisors
B. observe this employee at his work for a week shortly before you prepare the report
C. examine the employee's production records and compare them with the standards set for the position
D. obtain tactfully from his fellow employees their frank opinions of his work

24. Of the following, the CHIEF value of a flow of work chart to the management of an organization is its usefulness in 24.____

A. locating the causes of delay in carrying out an operation
B. training new employees in the performance of their duties
C. determining the effectiveness of the employees in the organization
D. determining the accuracy of its organization chart

25. Assume that a procedure for handling certain office forms has just been extensively revised. As supervisor of a small unit, you are to instruct your subordinates in the use of the new procedure, which is rather complicated. 25.____
Of the following, it would be LEAST helpful to your subordinates for you to

A. compare the revised procedure with the one it has replaced
B. state that you believe the revised procedure to be better than the one it has replaced

C. tell them that they will probably find it difficult to learn the new procedure
D. give only a general outline of the revised procedure at first and then follow with more detailed instructions

26. A supervisor may make assignments to his subordinates in the form of a command, a request, or a call for volunteers. 26.____
It is LEAST desirable for a supervisor to make an assignment in the form of a command when

A. a serious emergency has risen
B. an employee objects to carrying out an assignment
C. the assignment must be completed immediately
D. the assignment is an unpleasant one

27. For an office supervisor to confer periodically with his subordinates in order to anticipate job problems which are likely to arise is desirable MAINLY because 27.____

A. there will be fewer problems for which hasty decisions will have to be made
B. some problems which are anticipated may not arise
C. his subordinates will learn to refer the problems arising in the unit to him
D. constant anticipation of future problems tends to raise additional problems

28. A methods improvement program might be called a war against habit. 28.____
The MOST accurate implication of this statement is that

A. routine handling of routine office assignments should be discouraged
B. standardization of office procedures may encourage employees to form inefficient work habits
C. employees tend to continue the use of existing procedures, even when such procedures are inefficient
D. procedures should be changed constantly to prevent them from becoming habits

29. An office supervisor may give either a written or an oral order to his subordinates when making an assignment. 29.____
Of the following, it would be MOST appropriate for a supervisor to issue an order in writing when

A. a large number of two-page reports must be stapled together before the end of the day
B. the assignment is to be completed within two hours after it is issued to his subordinates
C. his subordinates have completed an identical assignment the day before
D. several entries must be made on a form at varying intervals of time by different clerks

30. A supervisor should always remember that the instruction or training of new employees is most effective if it is given when and where it is needed. 30.____
On the basis of this statement, it is MOST appropriate to conclude that

A. the new employee should be trained to handle any aspect of his work at the time he starts his job
B. the new employee should be given the training essential to get him started and additional training when he requires it

C. an employee who has received excessive training will be just as ineffective as one who has received inadequate training
D. a new employee is trained most effectively by his own supervisor

---

KEY (CORRECT ANSWERS)

1.	A	16.	B
2.	D	17.	C
3.	D	18.	B
4.	B	19.	C
5.	C	20.	B
6.	B	21.	A
7.	A	22.	B
8.	C	23.	C
9.	D	24.	A
10.	C	25.	C
11.	B	26.	D
12.	B	27.	A
13.	D	28.	C
14.	A	29.	D
15.	B	30.	B

TEST 2

DIRECTIONS: Each question or incomplete statement is followed by several suggested answers or completions. Select the one that BEST answers the question or completes the statement. *PRINT THE LETTER OF THE CORRECT ANSWER IN THE SPACE AT THE RIGHT.*

Questions 1-6.

DIRECTIONS: Each of Questions 1 through 6 consists of a statement which contains one word that is incorrectly used because it is not in keeping with the meaning that the statement is evidently intended to convey. For each of these questions, you are to select the INCORRECTLY used word and substitute for it one of the words lettered A, B, C, or D which helps best to convey the meaning of the statement. In the space at the right, print the capital letter preceding the word which should be substituted for the incorrectly used word.

1. The determination of the value of the employees in an organization is fundamental not only as a guide to the administration of salary schedules, promotion, demotion, and transfer, but also as a means of keeping the working force on its toes and of checking the originality of selection methods. 1.____

A. effectiveness
B. initiation
C. increasing
D. system

2. No training course can operate to full advantage without job descriptions which indicate training requirements so that those parts of the job requiring the most training can be carefully analyzed before the training course is completed. 2.____

A. improved
B. started
C. least
D. meet

3. The criticism that supervisors are discriminatory in their treatment of subordinates is, to some extent, untrue for the subjective nature of many supervisory decisions makes it probable that many employees who have not progressed will attribute their lack of success to supervisory favoritism. 3.____

A. knowledge
B. unavoidable
C. detrimental
D. deny

4. Some demands of employees will, if satisfied, result in a decrease in production. Some supervisors largely ignore such demands on the part of their subordinates, and instead concentrate on the direction and production of work; others yield to such requests and thereby emphasize the production goals and objectives set by higher levels of authority. 4.____

A. responsibility
B. increase
C. neglect
D. value

5. It is generally accepted that when a supervisor is at least as well informed about the work of his unit as are his subordinates, he will fail to win their approval, which is essential to him if he is to supervise the unit effectively. 5.____

A. unimportant
B. preferable
C. unless
D. attention

6. The laws of almost every state permit certain classes of persons to vote despite their absence from home at election time. Sometimes this privilege is given only to members of the armed forces of the United States, though more commonly it is extended to all voters whose occupations make absence preventable. 6.____

A. prohibition
B. sanction
C. intangible
D. necessary

Questions 7-9.

DIRECTIONS: Questions 7 through 9 are to be answered SOLELY on the basis of the information contained in the following statement.

The need for the best in management techniques has given rise to the expression *scientific management.* Within reasonable limits, management can be scientific, but it will probably be many decades before it becomes truly scientific either in the factory or in the office. As long as it is impossible to measure accurately individual performance and to equate human behavior, so long will it be impossible to develop completely scientific techniques of office management. There is a likelihood, of course, that management might be reduced to a science when it is applied to inanimate objects which facilitate operations, such as machinery, office equipment and furnishings, and forms. The limiting factor, therefore, is the human element.

7. The above statement is concerned PRIMARILY with the 7.____

A. value of scientific office management
B. methods for the development of scientific office management
C. need for the best office management techniques
D. possibility of reducing office management to a science

8. According to the above statement, the realization of truly scientific office management is dependent upon the 8.____

A. expression of management techniques
B. development of accurate personnel measurement techniques
C. passage of many decades, most probably
D. elimination of individual differences in human behavior

9. According to the above statement, the scientific management of inanimate objects 9.____

A. occurs automatically because there is no human factor
B. cannot occur in a factory, but can occur in an office
C. could be achieved without the concurrent achievement of truly scientific office management
D. is not a necessary component of truly scientific office management

Questions 10-12.

DIRECTIONS: Questions 10 through 12 are to be answered SOLELY on the basis of the information contained in the following statement.

The office was once considered as nothing more than a focal point of internal and external correspondence. It was capable only of dispatching a few letters upon occasion and of preparing records of little practical value. Under such a concept, the vitality of the office force was impaired. Initiative became stagnant, and the lot of the office worker was not likely to be a happy one. However, under the new concept of office management, the possibilities of waste and mismanagement in office operation are now fully recognized, as are the possibilities for the modern office to assist in the direction and control of business operations. Fortunately, the modern concept of the office as a centralized service-rendering unit is gaining ever greater acceptance in today's complex business world, for without the modern office, the production wheels do not turn and the distribution of goods and services is not possible.

10. According to the above statement, the fundamental difference between the old and the new concept of the office is the change in the 10.____

 A. accepted functions of the office
 B. content and the value of the records kept
 C. office methods and systems
 D. vitality and morale of the office force

11. According to the above statement, an office operated today under the old concept of the office MOST likely would 11.____

 A. make older workers happy in their jobs
 B. be part of an old thriving business concern
 C. have a passive role in the conduct of a business enterprise
 D. attract workers who do not believe in modern methods

12. Of the following, the MOST important implication of the above statement is that a present day business organization cannot function effectively without the 12.____

 A. use of modern office equipment
 B. participation and cooperation of the office
 C. continued modernization of office procedures
 D. employment of office workers with skill and initiative

Questions 13-31.

DIRECTIONS: Each of Questions 13 through 31 consists of a word in capitals followed by four suggested meanings of the word. Print in the space at the right the letter preceding the word which means MOST NEARLY the same as the word in capitals.

13. PREDILECTION 13.____

 A. prophecy B. preference
 C. memory D. resistance

14. INVETERATE 14.____

 A. inexperienced B. inhuman
 C. incapable D. confirmed

15. APATHETIC 15.____

 A. kind B. indifferent
 C. alert D. sorrowful

16. FRACTIOUS 16.____
    A. irritable B. partial C. typical D. sincere

17. EDIFICATION 17.____
    A. revision
    B. enlightenment
    C. act of complimenting
    D. promotion to higher office

18. PLENARY 18.____
    A. diplomatic
    B. executive
    C. preliminary
    D. full

19. TRUCULENT 19.____
    A. peaceful B. notorious C. fierce D. loud

20. VICARIOUS 20.____
    A. harmful
    B. supreme
    C. intentional
    D. substituted

21. EQUIVOCAL 21.____
    A. nominal B. noisy C. obstinate D. ambiguous

22. ANCILLARY 22.____
    A. compelling
    B. subsidiary
    C. primary
    D. authentic

23. CONTRAVENE 23.____
    A. postpone B. precede C. obstruct D. assemble

24. EPHEMERAL 24.____
    A. transitory
    B. fully satisfied
    C. deep
    D. mistaken

25. PLACATE 25.____
    A. appease B. locate C. conceal D. participate

26. IMPUTE 26.____
    A. calculate B. insult C. attribute D. invite

27. ANTITHESIS 27.____
    A. essence
    B. corruption
    C. infringement
    D. contrary

28. OFFICIOUS 28.____
    A. meddlesome
    B. effective
    C. arbitrary
    D. harsh

29. REMONSTRATE 29.____

A. present reasons in opposition
B. prove conclusively
C. show cause for concern
D. accept reluctantly

30. DIGRESS 30.____

A. resist
B. dictate
C. turn aside
D. come to a halt

31. STIPULATION 31.____

A. evaluation
B. decision
C. agreement
D. exception

Questions 32-40.

DIRECTIONS: Questions 32 through 40 are to be answered on the basis of the information contained in the four charts shown below which relate to a municipal department. These charts show for the fiscal year 2015-16 the total departmental expenditures for salaries for all its employees; the distribution of expenditures for salaries for permanent employees, by title; the distribution of all employees, both permanent and temporary, by title; and the distribution of temporary employees, by title.

Departmental Expenditures
For Salaries For Fiscal Year
Total: $129,000,000

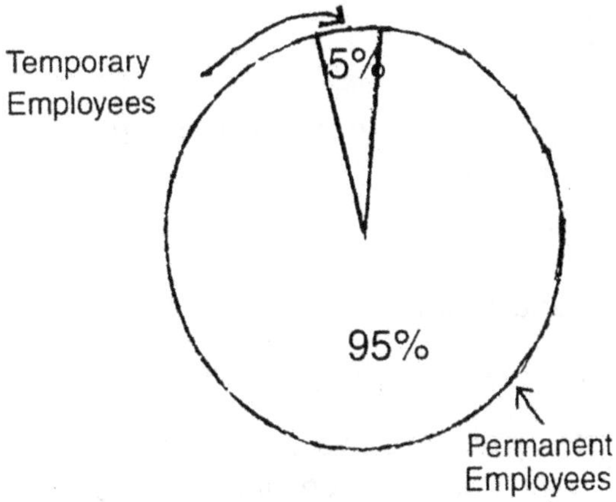

Distribution of Expenditures
For Salaries For Permanent
Employees, By Title

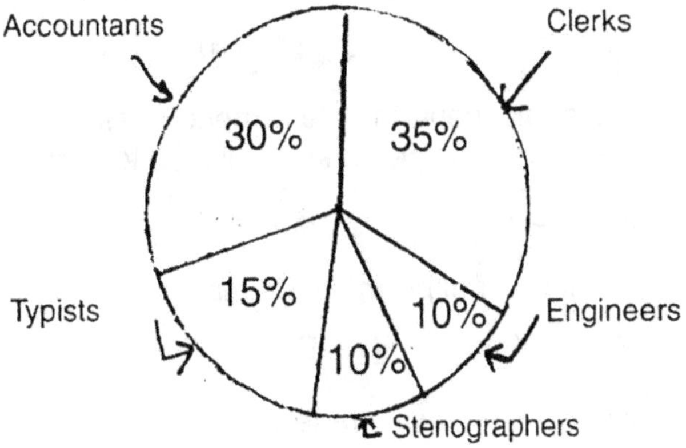

Distribution of All Employees,
Both Permanent and Temporary,
By Title
Total Number of Employees: 3,200

Distribution of Temporary
Employees, By Title
Total Number of Temporary
Employees: 150

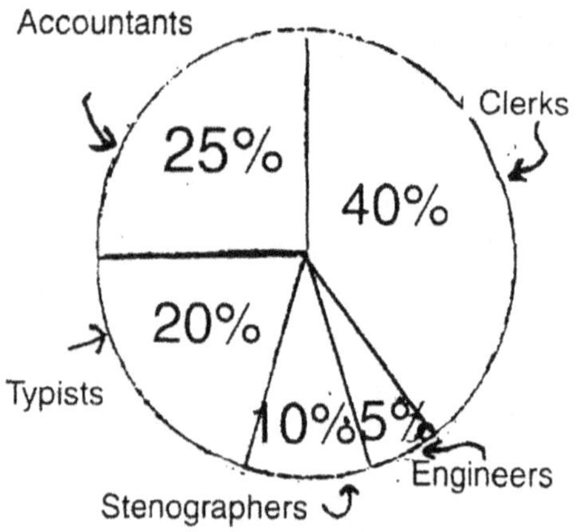

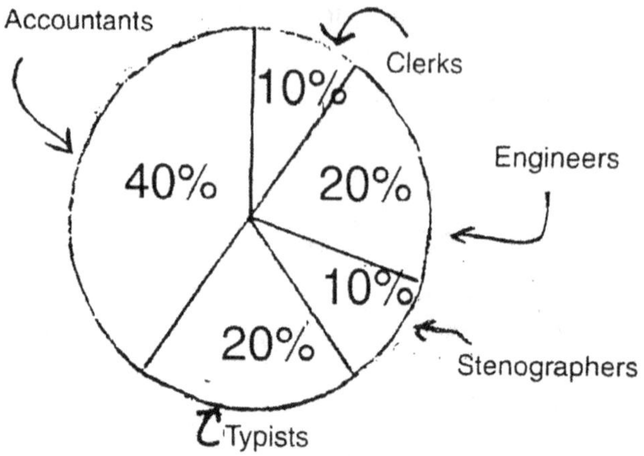

SAMPLE COMPUTATION:

The total amount of money expended for the salaries of all the permanent typists can be computed as follows:

By taking 95% of $129,000,000, the total amount of money expended for the salaries of all permanent employees can be obtained. The total amount of money expended for the salaries of all the permanent typists can then be obtained by taking 15% of the money expended for the salaries of all permanent employees. The answer is $18,382,500.

You may find it useful to arrange your computations on scratch paper in an orderly manner since the correct computations for one question may also be helpful in answering another question.

32. The TOTAL number of permanent typists is 32.____

A. 640 B. 670 C. 608 D. 610

33. Of the total departmental expenditures for salaries for both permanent and temporary employees, the percentage allotted to permanent clerks is MOST NEARLY 33.____

A. 25% B. 31% C. 33% D. 35%

34. The number of permanent employees who are NOT engineers is 34.____

A. 2,890 B. 3,070 C. 3,040 D. 2,920

35. Assume that the average annual salary of the temporary accountants is $40,000. Then the average annual salary of the permanent accountants exceeds the average annual salary of the temporary accountants by MOST NEARLY 35.____

A. 25% B. 20% C. 75% D. 40%

36. The average annual salary of the permanent clerks is MOST NEARLY 36.____

A. $33,300 B. $33,900 C. $35,250 D. $35,700

37. If the temporary stenographers receive 8 percent of the total salaries allotted to temporary employees, then the average annual salary of the temporary stenographers is MOST NEARLY 37.____

A. $34,500 B. $38,500 C. $36,000 D. $40,000

38. Assume that the temporary typists receive an average annual salary that is 3 percent less than the average annual salary that is paid to the permanent typists. Then the average annual salary of the temporary typist is MOST NEARLY 38.____

A. $27,850 B. $29,250 C. $30,000 D. $32,150

39. Assume that the average annual salary of the permanent engineers exceeds the average annual salary of the temporary engineers by $30,000. 39.____
Then the percentage of the total departmental expenditures for salaries for temporary employees that is allotted to temporary engineers is MOST NEARLY

A. 15% B. 20% C. 25% D. 30%

40. If one-half of the permanent accountants earn an average of $45,000 per annum, then the average annual salary of the other permanent accountants is MOST NEARLY 40.____

A. $51,150 B. $51,750 C. $54,350 D. $57,100

KEY (CORRECT ANSWERS)

1. A	11. C	21. D	31. C
2. B	12. B	22. B	32. D
3. B	13. B	23. C	33. C
4. C	14. D	24. A	34. D
5. C	15. B	25. A	35. A
6. D	16. A	26. C	36. B
7. D	17. B	27. D	37. A
8. B	18. D	28. A	38. B
9. C	19. C	29. A	39. D
10. A	20. D	30. C	40. C

EXAMINATION SECTION
TEST 1

DIRECTIONS: Each question or incomplete statement is followed by several suggested answers or completions. Select the one that BEST answers the question or completes the statement. *PRINT THE LETTER OF THE CORRECT ANSWER IN THE SPACE AT THE RIGHT.*

1. Assume that you have been placed in charge of a unit where the quality of the work performed is poor. You plan to discuss the matter of improving the quality of the work at a staff meeting of the unit. 1.____
Of the following courses of action which you might take at this meeting, the BEST one is to

   A. describe a few cases of exceptionally poor work performance, then have the employees performing this work explain why their work was done poorly
   B. inform the staff that you will be criticized by your own superior if the quality of the unit's work does not improve, then discuss, in general terms, the problem of improving the quality of the work
   C. discuss the problem of improving the quality of the unit's work, then call upon each employee by name for his suggestions for improving the work he performs
   D. present the problem to the staff, then indicate and discuss specific methods for improving the quality of the work

2. The competent supervisor realizes that procedures which have been followed for a considerable length of time can frequently be reconstructed and improved. He knows that charts, or diagrams, are often of inestimable value in bringing out forcibly and visibly the outstanding defects in a procedure. 2.____
Of the following types of charts, the one which would ordinarily be of MOST value to a supervisor making a study of the clerical procedures in his unit is a(n) ______ chart.

   A. organization
   B. circle or pie
   C. flow or process
   D. bar or column

3. Assume that you have received a letter requesting certain information. You know that the time required to obtain this information may extend from several days to several weeks. You may take either of two courses of action in replying to this letter. You may withhold your reply until the requested information has been obtained, or you may acknowledge immediately the receipt of the letter and send the information when it has been obtained. 3.____
For you to take the FIRST rather than the second course of action would be

   A. *desirable;* you will thus reduce the amount of correspondence
   B. *undesirable;* a person requesting information should be informed as soon as possible that his request has been received and that it will be attended to
   C. *desirable;* if the information should be obtained within a few days, it would appear wasteful and ridiculous to have sent two letters in so short a period of time
   D. *undesirable;* some letters do not require any response at all

4. In an office where applicants for employment are interviewed, it is MOST desirable that the office furniture be arranged so that the 4.____

A. person being interviewed is seated where he can see the notes being recorded by the interviewer
B. person being interviewed cannot be seen by other interviewers
C. conversation between the interviewer and the person being interviewed cannot be overheard by others
D. interviewer faces the person being interviewed but has his back to others who are waiting to be interviewed

5. Of the following factors, the one which is of LEAST importance in determining the number of subordinates that an individual should be assigned to supervise is the 5.____

A. nature of the work being supervised
B. qualifications of the individual as a supervisor
C. capabilities of the subordinates
D. lines of promotion for the subordinates

6. Suppose that a large number of semi-literate residents of this city have been requesting the assistance of your department. You are asked to prepare a form which these applicants will be required to fill out before their requests will be considered. 6.____
In view of these facts, the one of the following factors to which you should give the GREATEST amount of consideration in preparing this form is the

A. size of the form
B. sequence of the information asked for on the form
C. level of difficulty of the language used in the form
D. number of times which the form will have to be reviewed

7. Suppose that the employees in your unit are required to perform a great deal of computation involving a large amount of addition and subtraction. Since accuracy is more important than speed in the work of your unit, employees are required to check all the figures used in the computations before turning in their work. 7.____
Of the following machines, the one which would be MOST practicable for the work of your unit is a

A. listing adding machine
B. comptometer
C. punch card tabulating machine
D. billing machine

8. A supervisor is frequently required to prepare various types of written reports. 8.____
The one of the following features which is LEAST desirable in a lengthy report is that

A. the style of writing should be readable, interesting, and impersonal; it should not be too scholarly, nor make use of involved sentence structure
B. recommendations and conclusions resulting from the facts incorporated in the body of the report must appear only at the end of the report so that readers can follow the writer's line of reasoning
C. in determining the extent of technical detail and terminology to be used in the presentation of supporting data, such as charts, tables, graphs, case examples, etc., the technical knowledge of the prospective reader or readers should be kept in mind

D. the body of the report should mention all the pertinent facts and develop the writer's ideas in such a way that the recommendations will be a logical outgrowth of the arguments presented

9. Your department plans to install a suggestion box into which its employees may place their suggestions for improving departmental policies and procedures. As a reward for submitting a practical suggestion, additional vacation allowance will be granted to the author of each suggestion. The amount of additional vacation allowed will depend upon the value of the suggestion, as determined by a panel of judges. 9.____
To institute a procedure whereby the identity of the author will be concealed from the judges by the secretary of the department until the value of the suggestion has been determined would be

A. *undesirable;* many employees will refrain from making suggestions if they know that the suggestion will be judged anonymously
B. *desirable;* many employees will be encouraged to be frank and outspoken in their criticism; such a straightforward criticism is of more value to a department than suggestions for improvement
C. *undesirable;* if a suggestion is not clearly presented, the judges will be unable to obtain clarifying information from the author
D. *desirable;* it provides for strict impartiality in judging the worth of an idea and may thus encourage employee participation in the plan

10. The one of the following which should be considered the LEAST important objective of the city's service rating system is to 10.____

A. rate the employees on the basis of their potential abilities
B. establish a basis for assigning employees to special types of work
C. provide a means for recognizing superior work performance
D. reveal the need for training as well as the effectiveness of a training program

11. Instead of directing his attention solely toward devising new systems and procedures for performing established clerical operations, the alert office manager carefully studies these operations with a view to determining the value that accrues to the organization from their performance. 11.____
Of the following, the MOST valid implication of this statement is that

A. established clerical operations may not be of sufficient benefit to the organization to justify their continuance
B. devising new systems of performing clerical operations is no longer the function of the office manager
C. the performance of established clerical operations usually brings little or no direct benefit to an organization
D. devising better ways of performing a necessary clerical task may be of no value to an organization

12. A budget is a plan whereby a goal is set for future operations. It affords a medium for comparing actual expenditures with planned expenditures. 12.____
The one of the following which is the MOST accurate statement on the basis of this statement is that

A. the budget serves as an accurate measure of past as well as future expenditures
B. the budget presents an estimate of expenditures to be made in the future

C. budget estimates should be based upon past budget requirements
D. planned expenditures usually fall short of actual expenditures

13. Suppose that you are placed in charge of a unit in your department. You find that many of the employees have been disregarding the staff regulation requiring employees to be at their desks at 9:05 A.M. 13.____
Of the following, the LEAST desirable course of action for you to take would be to

A. call a meeting of the staff and explain why it is essential that all employees be at their desks at 9:05 A.M.
B. post conspicuously on the bulletin board a notice calling the employees' attention to the frequent violation of this regulation and requesting them to observe this regulation
C. recommend an above-average service rating for all employees who consistently comply with this regulation
D. summon the offenders and explain to them how their violation of this regulation results in decreasing the efficiency of the unit

14. Suppose that certain office responsibilities require you to be frequently absent from the unit you supervise. You have, therefore, decided to designate one of your staff members to act as unit head in your absence. 14.____
Of the following factors, the one which is MOST important in selecting the employee best fitted for this assignment is his

A. manner and personal appearance
B. estimated ability to perform work of a supervisory nature
C. ability to perform his present duties
D. relative seniority in the service

15. One of the assignments in the unit you supervise is the checking of a list of 500 unalphabetized names against an alphabetical 5x8 card index containing several thousand names. The clerk performing this task is to make sure that there is a card in the file for each name on the list. 15.____
The one of the following which you should suggest as the BEST procedure for the clerk to follow is for him to

A. rewrite the names on the list in alphabetical order, look for the corresponding card in the file, and place a check mark next to each name on the list for which he finds a card
B. take each name on the list in turn, look for the corresponding card in the file, and place a check mark in the corner of each card he finds
C. go through all the cards in the file in consecutive order and place a check mark next to each name on the list for which he finds a card
D. take each name on the list in turn, look for the corresponding card in the file, and place a check mark next to each name for which he finds a card

16. Suppose that you are in charge of a unit which maintains a rather intricate filing system. A new file clerk has been added to your staff. 16.____
Of the following assignments that may be given to this clerk, the one which requires the LEAST amount of knowledge of the filing system is

A. placing material in the files
B. removing papers from the files

C. classifying and coding material for filing
D. keeping a record of material taken from, and returned to, the files

17. In undertaking to improve the method of performing a certain job or operation, the new office manager should FIRST ascertain the 17.____

A. present method of performing the job
B. purpose of the job
C. number and titles of employees assigned to the job
D. methods used by other agencies to perform the same kind of job

18. The proofreading of a large number of reports has been assigned to two clerks. These clerks have been instructed to indicate all necessary corrections on a slip of paper, attach this correction slip to the reports, and send them to the typist for correction. 18.____
Of the following additional steps that might be taken before sending the reports to the typist, the BEST one is that the

A. clerks should proofread each report in its entirety after the corrections have been made on it
B. typist should make the necessary corrections and return the correction slip and the corrected reports to the clerks; the clerks should then examine the reports to see that all the requested corrections have been made properly
C. typist should make the necessary corrections, placing a check mark opposite each correction noted on the correction slip; she should then review the correction slip to make sure that no correction has been omitted
D. typist should make the necessary corrections, place a check mark opposite each correction noted on the correction slip, and return the reports and the correction slip to the clerks; the clerks should then review the correction slip to make sure that a check mark has been placed opposite each item on the correction slip

19. Suppose you are the supervisor of a unit in a city department. You notice that a clerk with long service in the department is arguing with a recently appointed clerk regarding the procedure to be followed in performing a certain task. Each is convinced he is right. The argument is disturbing the other employees. 19.____
Of the following, the BEST action for you to take in dealing with this problem is to

A. call the clerks to your desk, discuss the matter with them, and then state which procedure is the correct one
B. support the employee with the longer service, for to do otherwise will impair the morale of the office
C. call the clerks to your desk and tell them to settle their differences without disturbing the others
D. order the clerks to discontinue their argument immediately and to bring the matter up at the next staff conference, where the staff will determine which procedure is the correct one

20. Assume that you have devised a new procedure which you expected would result in a substantial reduction in the amount of paper used in performing the work of the unit you supervise. After trying out this new procedure in your unit for several weeks, you find that the quantity of paper saved is considerably less than you anticipated. 20.____
Of the following, the BEST action for you to take first is to

A. inform your staff that they are probably using paper unnecessarily and that in view of the current paper shortage, you expect them to conserve paper as much as possible
B. suspend the use of this new procedure until you can discover why it has not worked out as you anticipated
C. invite your subordinates to submit suggestions as to how the procedure may be improved
D. analyze the various processes involved in the new procedure to determine whether there are any factors which you may have overlooked

21. Assume that you are the head of the bureau of information in a city department. You are faced with the problem of replacing the clerk assigned to the information desk. Of the following available employees, the one who should be given the assignment is 21.____

A. John Jones, a new clerk who specialized in English at college and recently received a Master of Arts degree; at present, he has no permanent assignment
B. Mary Smith, an excellent stenographer who has had much experience as secretary to one of the bureau heads; she is intelligent, pleasant in manner, and learns quickly
C. Richard Roe, a clerk who has been rated as *tactful, dependable,* and *resourceful* by the various bureau heads who have prepared his service rating reports during the four years that he has been in the department
D. Jane Doe, who is a diligent typist when she works alone but who disturbs the other typists by her constant stream of chatter when she works near them

22. The one of the following which is the MOST accurate statement regarding routine operations in an office is that 22.____

A. routine assignments should not last more than two or three days each week
B. methods for performing routine work should be standardized as much as is practicable
C. routine work performed by one employee should be checked by another employee
D. changes in the procedures of a unit should not affect the existing routine operations of the unit

23. Modern management realizes the importance of sound personnel practices in business administration. It has found that production is largely dependent upon the effective utilization of an employee's interests, capabilities, and skills. Of the following, the MOST logical implication of the above statement is that 23.____

A. there should be one bureau in each business organization to take charge of both production and personnel administration
B. production cannot be increased without the utilization of a sound personnel policy
C. production will increase if the number of persons assigned to work in a business organization is increased
D. maximum efficiency in an organization cannot be achieved without proper placement of employees

24. In a city agency, 80 percent of the total number of employees are more than 25 years of age and 65 percent of the total number of employees are high school graduates. The SMALLEST possible percent of employees who are both high school graduates and more than 25 years of age is 24.____

A. 35% B. 45% C. 55% D. 65%

25. Two clerical units, X and Y, each having a different number of clerks, are assigned to file registration cards. It takes Unit X, which contains 8 clerks, 21 days to file the same number of cards that Unit Y can file in 28 days. It is also a fact that Unit X can file 174,528 cards in 72 days. Assuming that all the clerks in both units work at the same rate of speed, the number of cards which can be filed by Unit Y in 144 days, if 4 more clerks are added to the staff of Unit Y, is MOST NEARLY 25.____

A. 349,000 B. 436,000 C. 523,000 D. 669,000

KEY (CORRECT ANSWERS)

1.	D	11.	A
2.	C	12.	B
3.	B	13.	C
4.	C	14.	B
5.	D	15.	D
6.	C	16.	D
7.	A	17.	B
8.	B	18.	B
9.	D	19.	A
10.	A	20.	D

21. C
22. B
23. D
24. B
25. B

TEST 2

DIRECTIONS: Each question or incomplete statement is followed by several suggested answers or completions. Select the one that BEST answers the question or completes the statement. *PRINT THE LETTER OF THE CORRECT ANSWER IN THE SPACE AT THE RIGHT.*

Questions 1-5.

DIRECTIONS: Each of Questions 1 through 5 consists of a statement containing five words in capital letters. One of these words in capital letters is not in keeping with the meaning which the statement is evidently intended to carry. The five words in capital letters in each statement are reprinted after the statement. In the space at the right, print the capital letter preceding the one of the five words which does MOST to spoil the true meaning of the statement.

1. Within each major DIVISION in a properly set up public or private organization, provision is made so that each NECESSARY activity is CARED for and lines of AUTHORITY and responsibility are clear-cut and INFINITE. 1._____

   A. Division B. Necessary C. Cared
   D. Authority E. Infinite

2. In public service, the scale of salaries paid must be INCIDENTAL to the services rendered, with due CONSIDERATION for the attraction of the desired MANPOWER and for the MAINTENANCE of a standard of living COMMENSURATE with the work to be performed. 2._____

   A. Incidental B. Consideration C. Manpower
   D. Maintenance E. Commensurate

3. An understanding of the AIMS of an organization by the staff will AID greatly in increasing the DEMAND of the correspondence work of the office, and will to a large extent DETERMINE the NATURE of the correspondence. 3._____

   A. Aims B. Aid C. Demand
   D. Determine E. Nature

4. BECAUSE the Civil Service Commission strongly feels that the MERIT system is a key factor in the MAINTENANCE of democratic government, it has adopted as one of its major DEFENSES the progressive democratization of its own PROCEDURES in dealing with candidates for positions in the public service. 4._____

   A. Because B. Merit C. Maintenance
   D. Defenses E. Procedures

5. Retirement and pensions systems are ESSENTIAL not only to provide employees with a means of support in the future, but also to prevent longevity and CHARITABLE considerations from UPSETTING the PROMOTIONAL opportunities for RETIRED members of the career service. 5._____

   A. Essential B. Charitable C. Upsetting
   D. Promotional E. Retired

6. Assume that two machines, each costing $5900, were purchased for your office. Each machine requires the services of an operator at a salary of $800 per month. These machines are to replace six clerks, two of whom earn $620 per month each, and four of whom earn $680 per month each.
The number of months it will take for the cost of the machines to be made up from the savings in salaries is 6.____

A. less than four months
B. four months
C. five months
D. more than five months

7. Suppose that the amount of stationery used by your department in August decreased by 16% as compared with the amount used in July, and that the amount used in September increased by 25% as compared with the amount used in August.
The amount of stationery used in September as compared with the amount used in July is 7.____

A. greater by 5 percent
B. less by 5 percent
C. greater by 9 percent
D. the same

8. This letter appears to have been written by some *indigent* person.
The word *indigent,* as used in this sentence, means MOST NEARLY 8.____

A. foreign-born
B. needy
C. uneducated
D. angry

9. The conference began under *auspicious* circumstances.
The word *auspicious,* as used in this sentence, means MOST NEARLY 9.____

A. favorable
B. chaotic
C. questionable
D. threatening

10. An *inordinate* amount of work was assigned to the newly appointed clerk.
The word *inordinate,* as used in this sentence, means MOST NEARLY 10.____

A. unanticipated
B. adequate
C. inexcusable
D. excessive

11. The report which was obtained *surreptitiously* was very detailed and fully documented.
The word *surreptitiously,* as used in this sentence, means MOST NEARLY 11.____

A. stealthily
B. a short time ago
C. with great difficulty
D. unexpectedly

12. We all knew him to be a man of *probity.*
The word *probity,* as used in this sentence, means MOST NEARLY 12.____

A. culture
B. proven ability
C. integrity
D. dignity and poise

13. He made a *cursory* study of the problem before starting on the assignment.
The word *cursory,* as used in this sentence, means MOST NEARLY 13.____

A. detailed
B. secret
C. hasty
D. methodical

14. The regulation had a *salutary* effect upon the members of the staff.
The word *salutary,* as used in this sentence, means MOST NEARLY 14.____

A. disturbing
B. beneficial
C. confusing
D. premature

15. The *solicitous* supervisor discussed the employees' grievances with them. The word *solicitous,* as used in this sentence, means MOST NEARLY 15.____

A. concerned
B. impartial
C. wise
D. experienced

16. The employee *categorically* denied all responsibility for the error. The word *categorically,* as used in this sentence, means MOST NEARLY 16.____

A. repeatedly
B. loudly
C. hesitantly
D. absolutely

17. No *stipend* was specified in the agreement. The word *stipend,* as used in this sentence, means MOST NEARLY 17.____

A. statement of working conditions
B. receipt for payment
C. compensation for services
D. delivery date

18. A clerk who comes across the abbreviation *viz.* should know that it stands for 18.____

A. by way of
B. in the same place
C. volume number
D. namely

Questions 19-25.

DIRECTIONS: Questions 19 through 25 are to be answered SOLELY on the basis of the following information.

Assume that the following regulations were established in your department to compute vacation allowances for services rendered by its employees during the period from June 1, 2014 through May 31, 2015. You are to determine the answer to each of the questions on the basis of these regulations.

VACATION REGULATIONS
(for the period June 1, 2014 - May 31, 2015)
The vacation allowance for this period is to be taken after May 31, 2015.

Standard Vacation Allowance

Permanent per annum employees shall be granted 25 days vacation for a full year's service in such status. Employees who have served less than a full year in a permanent per annum status shall receive an allowance of 2 days for each month of such service.

Per diem employees shall be granted 1 1/2 days vacation for each month of service in such status.

Temporary employees shall be granted one day of vacation for each month of service in such status.

No vacation credit shall accrue to employees for the time they are on leave of absence.

Additional Allowance for Overtime

One day of vacation allowance shall be granted for each seven hours of accrued overtime. Where there is a balance of less than 7 hours of accrued overtime, one-half day of vacation shall be granted for each 3 1/2 hours of such overtime. In no case shall the additional vacation allowed for accrued overtime exceed 6 days.

Deductions for Excessive Sick Leave

Sick leave allowance for all employees, regardless of length of service, shall be 12 days for the year. Sick leave taken in excess of 12 days shall be deducted from vacation allowance. Any unused sick leave balance will be canceled on May 31, 2015.

Deductions for Excessive Lateness

Deductions for excessive lateness shall be made from vacation allowance in accordance with the following schedule:

No. of Times Late	Deduction From Vacation Allowance
0- 50	no deduction
51- 60	1/2 day
61- 70	1 day
71- 80	1 1/2 days
81- 90	2 days
91- 100	2 1/2 days
101- 120	4 days
121- 140	6 days
141 or over	penalty to be determined by Secretary of Department

Unused Vacation

Unused vacation allowance earned during the previous year shall be added to the current vacation allowance, up to a maximum of twelve days.

19. Employee A served as a temporary employee from June 1, 2014 through January 31, 2015, and as a permanent per annum employee from February 1, 2015 through May 31, 2015. During the year, he accumulated 45 1/2 hours of overtime and was late 65 times. His vacation allowance should be ______ days. 19.____

A. 16 B. 15 C. 21 1/2 D. 21

20. Employee B was newly appointed to the department as a per diem employee on September 1, 2014. During the year, he took 15 days of sick leave and was late 48 times. His vacation allowance should be ______ days. 20.____

A. less than 10
B. 10 1/2
C. 15
D. 12 1/2

21. Employee C has been a permanent per annum employee throughout the year. He had 15 days of vacation due him from the previous year. During the year, he was late 85 times, he took 10 days of sick leave, and he accumulated 38 1/2 hours of overtime. His vacation allowance should be ______ days. 21.____

A. 38 1/2
B. 42 1/2
C. 40 1/2
D. more than 43

22. Employee D was newly appointed to the department as a permanent per annum employee on July 1, 2014. He was on leave of absence from December 1, 2014 through February 28, 2015. During the year, he took 6 days of sick leave, he was late 70 times, and he accumulated 21 hours of overtime. 22.___
His vacation allowance should be ______ days.

A. 24 B. 18 C. 17 1/2 D. 19 1/2

23. Employee E served as a per diem employee from June 1, 2014 through July 31, 2014, and as a permanent per annum employee from August 1, 2014 to May 31, 2015. He had 6 days of vacation due him from the previous year. During the year, he took 13 days of sick leave, he accumulated 70 days of overtime, and he was late 132 times. 23.___
His vacation allowance should be ______ days.

A. less than 29
B. 29
C. 30
D. more than 30

24. The MAXIMUM total vacation allowance which a permanent per annum employee can have due him by May 31, 2015 is ______ days. 24.___

A. 43 B. 25 C. 31 D. 37

25. An employee who has served as a temporary employee for 6 months and as a permanent per annum employee for 6 months will earn exactly 25.___

A. two-thirds as much vacation as an employee who has been on a permanent per annum basis for the whole year
B. as much vacation as an employee who has been on a per diem basis for the whole year
C. as much vacation as an employee who has been on a per diem basis for 4 months and on a permanent per annum basis for 8 months
D. as much vacation as an employee who has been on a per diem basis for 8 months and on a permanent per annum basis for 4 months

KEY (CORRECT ANSWERS)

1. E
2. A
3. C
4. D
5. E
6. C
7. A
8. B
9. A
10. D
11. A
12. C
13. C
14. B
15. A
16. D
17. C
18. D
19. D
20. B
21. C
22. B
23. A
24. A
25. B

EXAMINATION SECTION
TEST 1

DIRECTIONS: Each question or incomplete statement is followed by several suggested answers or completions. Select the one that BEST answers the question or completes the statement. *PRINT THE LETTER OF THE CORRECT ANSWER IN THE SPACE AT THE RIGHT.*

1. As head of the filing unit in your department, you have been receiving complaints that material which should be in the files cannot be located. On investigating this matter, you find that one of your new clerks has been careless in placing material in the files. The BEST of the following actions which you might take FIRST is to 1.____

   A. admonish this clerk and tell him that he will be given a below-average service rating if his carelessness continues
   B. remind this clerk that he is a probationary employee and that his services may be terminated at the end of his probationary period if his carelessness continues
   C. call the attention of this clerk to the effects of filing and impress upon him the necessity for accuracy in filing
   D. give this clerk another assignment in the unit where accuracy is less essential

2. The GREATEST amount of improvement in the efficiency and morale of a unit will be brought about by the supervisor who 2.____

   A. reminds his employees constantly that they must follow departmental regulations
   B. frequently praises an employee in the presence of the other employees in the unit
   C. invariably gives mild reproof and constructive criticism to subordinates when he discovers that they have made a mistake
   D. assigns duties to employees in conformance with their abilities and interests as far as practicable

3. Assume that you are the supervisor of a unit which performs routine clerical work. For you to encourage your subordinates to make suggestions for increasing the efficiency of the unit is 3.____

   A. *undesirable;* employees who perform routine work may resent having additional duties and responsibilities assigned to them
   B. *desirable;* by presenting criticism of each other's work, the employees may develop a competitive spirit and in this way increase their efficiency
   C. *undesirable*; the employees may conclude that the supervisor is not capable of efficiently supervising the work of the unit
   D. *desirable*; increased interest in their assignment may be acquired by the employees, and the work of the unit may be performed more efficiently

4. The MOST accurate of the following statements regarding the chief purpose for maintaining a perpetual inventory of office supplies is that it 4.____

   A. eliminates the necessity for making a physical inventory of office supplies
   B. makes available at all times a record of the balance of office supplies on hand
   C. reduces the amount of clerical work required in distributing supplies
   D. reduces the amount of paper work involved in requisitioning supplies

5. Of the following, a centralized filing system is LEAST suitable for filing 5.____

A. material which is confidential in nature
B. routine correspondence
C. periodic reports of the divisions of the department
D. material used by several divisions of the department

6. Form letters should be used mainly when 6.____

A. an office has to reply to a great many similar inquiries
B. the type of correspondence varies widely
C. it is necessary to have letters which are well-phrased and grammatically correct
D. letters of inquiry have to be answered as soon as possible after they are received

7. Assume that you have recommended that one of your subordinates be given a below-average service rating. The subordinate disagreed with your recommendation and requests that you discuss the service rating report with him. 7.____
In taking up this matter with the employee, the BEST of the following procedures for you to follow is to

A. discuss the general standards of evaluation you have used, rather than his specific deficiencies
B. tell him that it would be too time-consuming to discuss his report with him, but inform him that objective standards were used in evaluating all employees and that the reports will be reviewed by an impartial board which will make any changes it deems necessary
C. explain the standards of evaluation you have used and discuss this subordinate's work with him in relation to these standards
D. point out to your subordinate that you are in a better position than he to compare his work with that of the other employees in your unit

8. Suppose that you are assigned to prepare a form from which certain information will be posted in a ledger. It would be MOST helpful to the person posting the information in the ledger if, in designing the form, you were to 8.____

A. use the same color paper for both the form and the ledger
B. make the form the same size as the pages of the ledger
C. have the information on the form in the same order as that used in the ledger
D. include in the form a box which is to be initialed when the data on the form have been posted in the ledger

9. A misplaced record is a lost record. 9.____
Of the following, the MOST valid implication of this statement in regard to office work is that

A. all records in an office should be filed in strict alphabetical order
B. accuracy in filing is essential
C. only one method of filing should be used throughout the office
D. files should be locked when not in use

10. John Smith is applying for a provisional appointment as a clerk in your department. He presents a letter of recommendation from a former employer stating: *John Smith was rarely late or absents he has a very pleasing manner, and never got into an argument with his fellow employees.* 10.____
The above information concerning this applicant

A. proves clearly that he produces more work than the average employee
B. indicates that he was probably attempting to conceal his inefficiency from his former employer
C. presents no conclusive evidence of his ability to do clerical work
D. indicates clearly that with additional training he will make a good supervisor

11. It is not possible to draw a hard and fast line between training courses for greater efficiency on the present job. 11.____
This statement means MOST NEARLY that

A. to be worthwhile, a training course should prepare the employee for promotion as well as for greater efficiency on the present job
B. training courses should be designed only to increase employee efficiency on the present job
C. training courses should be given only to employees who are competing for promotion
D. by attending a training course for promotion, employees may become more efficient in their present work

12. Approximate figures serve as well as exact figures to indicate trends and make comparisons. 12.____
Of the following, the MOST accurate statement on the basis of this statement is that

A. it takes less time to obtain approximate figures than exact figures
B. exact figures are rarely used as they require too much computation
C. for certain purposes, approximate figures are as revealing as exact figures
D. approximate figures can usually be used in place of exact figures

13. Suppose that you are placed in charge of a unit in your department. You find that many of the employees have been disregarding the staff regulation requiring employees to be at their desks at 9:05 A.M. 13.____
Of the following, the LEAST desirable course of action for you to take would be to

A. call a meeting of the staff and explain why it is essential that all employees be at their desks at 9:05 A.M.
B. post conspicuously on the bulletin board a notice calling the employees' attention to the frequent violation of this regulation and requesting them to observe this regulation
C. recommend an above-average service rating for all employees who consistently comply with this regulation, provided their work is satisfactory
D. summon the offenders and explain to them how their violation of this regulation results in decreasing the efficiency of the unit

14. Suppose that certain office responsibilities require you to be frequently absent from the unit you supervise. You have, therefore, decided to designate one of your staff members to act as unit head in your absence. 14.____
Of the following factors, the one which is MOST important in selecting the employee best fitted for this assignment is his

A. manner and personal appearance
B. estimated ability to perform work of a supervisory nature
C. ability to perform his present duties
D. relative seniority in the service

15. One of the assignments in the unit you supervise is the checking of a list of 500 unalphabetized names against an alphabetical 5x8 card index containing several thousand names. The clerk performing this task is to make sure that there is a card in the file for each name on the list. 15.____
The one of the following which you should suggest as the BEST procedure for the clerk to follow is for him to

A. rewrite the names on the list in alphabetical order, look for the corresponding card in the file, and place a check mark next to each name on the list for which he finds a card
B. take each name on the list in turn, look for the corresponding card in the file, and place a check mark in the corner of each card he finds
C. go through all the cards in the file in consecutive order and place a check mark next to each name on the list for which he finds a card
D. take each name on the list in turn, look for the corresponding card in the file, and place a check mark next to each name on the list for which he finds a card

16. Suppose that you are in charge of a unit which maintains a rather intricate filing system. A new file clerk has been added to your staff. 16.____
Of the following assignments that may be given to this clerk, the one which requires the LEAST amount of knowledge of the filing system is

A. placing material in the files
B. removing papers from the files
C. classifying and coding material for filing
D. keeping a record of material taken from, and returned to, the files

17. In undertaking to improve the method of performing a certain job or operation, the new office manager should first ascertain the 17.____

A. present method of performing the job
B. purpose of the job
C. number and titles of employees assigned to the job
D. methods used by other agencies to perform the same kind of job

18. The proofreading of a large number of papers has been assigned to two clerks. These clerks have been instructed to indicate all necessary corrections on a slip of paper, attach this correction slip to the papers, and send them to the typist for correction. 18.____
Of the following additional steps that might be taken before sending the papers to the xerox operator, the BEST one is that the

A. clerks should proofread each paper in its entirety after the corrections have been made on it
B. typist should make the necessary corrections and return the correction slip and the corrected papers to the clerks; the clerks should then examine the papers to see that all the requested corrections have been made properly
C. typist should make the necessary corrections, placing a check mark opposite each correction noted on the correction slip; she should then review the correction slip to make sure that no correction has been omitted
D. typist should make the necessary corrections, place a check mark opposite each correction noted on the correction slip, and return the papers and the correction slip to the clerks; the clerks should then review the correction slip to make sure that a check mark has been placed opposite each item on the correction slip

19. Suppose you are the supervisor of a unit in a department. You notice that a clerk with long service in the department is arguing with a recently appointed clerk regarding the procedure to be followed in performing a certain task. Each is convinced he is right. The argument is disturbing the other employees. 19.____
Of the following, the BEST action for you to take in dealing with this problem is to

A. call the clerks to your desk, discuss the matter with them, and then state which procedure is the correct one
B. support the employee with the longer service, for to do otherwise will impair the morale of the office
C. call the clerks to your desk and tell them to settle their differences without disturbing the others
D. order the clerks to discontinue their argument immediately and to bring the matter up at the next staff conference, where the staff will determine which procedure is the correct one

20. Assume that you devised a new procedure which you expected would result in a substantial reduction in the amount of paper used in performing the work of the unit you supervise. After trying out this new procedure in your unit for several weeks, you find that the quantity of paper saved is considerably less than you anticipated. 20.____
Of the following, the BEST action for you to take first is to

A. inform your staff that they are probably using paper unnecessarily, and that in view of the current paper shortage, you expect them to conserve paper as much as possible
B. suspend the use of this new procedure until you can discover why it has not worked out as you anticipated
C. invite your subordinates to submit suggestions as to how the procedure may be improved
D. analyze the various processes involved in the new procedure to determine whether there are any factors which you may have overlooked

21. Assume that you are the head of the bureau of information in a department. You are faced with the problem of replacing the clerk assigned to the information desk. 21.____
Of the following available employees, the one who should be given the assignment is

A. John Jones, a new clerk who specialized in English at college and recently received a Master of Arts degree; at present, he has no permanent assignment
B. Mary Smith, an excellent stenographer who has had much experience as secretary to one of the bureau heads; she is intelligent, pleasant in manner, and learns quickly
C. Richard Roe, a clerk who has been rated as *tactful, dependable,* and *resourceful* by the various bureau heads who have prepared his service rating reports during the four years that he has been in the department
D. Jane Doe, who is a diligent typist when she works alone but who disturbs the other typists by her constant stream of chatter when she works near them

22. The one of the following which is the MOST accurate statement regarding routine operations in an office is that 22.____

A. routine assignments should not last more than two or three days each week
B. methods for performing routine work should be standardized as much as is practicable
C. routine work performed by one employee should be checked by another employee
D. changes in the procedures of a unit should not affect the existing routine operations of the unit

23. Modern management realizes the importance of sound personnel practices in business administration. It has found that production is largely dependent upon the effective utilization of an employee's interests, capabilities, and skills. 23.____
Of the following, the MOST logical implication of the above statement is that

A. there should be one bureau in each business organization to take charge of both production and personnel administration
B. production cannot be increased without the utilization of a sound personnel policy
C. production will increase if the number of persons assigned to work in a business organization is increased
D. maximum efficiency in an organization cannot be achieved without proper placement of employees

24. One of the stenographers under your supervision has completed all of her assignments, and there is no additional typing to be done. 24.____
It would be LEAST desirable for you to suggest that she

A. straighten up the supply cabinet to improve its appearance
B. check the files for material that is surplus or outdated
C. read the daily newspaper to keep up with current events
D. practice shorthand or typing to improve her speed

25. Of the following, the BEST way for a supervisor to determine when further on-the-job training in a particular work area is needed is by 25.____

A. evaluating the employees' work performance
B. asking the employees
C. determining the ratio of idle time to total work time
D. classifying the jobs in the work area

Questions 26-30.

DIRECTIONS: Each of Questions 26 through 30 consists of a statement containing five words in capital letters. One of these words in capital letters is not in keeping with the meaning which the statement is evidently intended to carry. The five words in capital letters in each statement are reprinted after the statement. In the space at the right, write the letter preceding the one of the five words which does most to spoil the true meaning of the statement.

26. Within each major DIVISION in a properly set-up public or private organization, provision is made so that each NECESSARY activity is CARED for and lines of AUTHORITY and responsibility are clear-cut and INFINITE. 26.____

A. division B. necessary C. cared
D. authority E. infinite

27. In public service, the scale of salaries paid must be INCIDENTAL to the services rendered, with due CONSIDERATION for the attraction of the desired MANPOWER and for the MAINTENANCE of a standard of living COMMENSURATE with the work to be performed. 27.____

A. incidental B. consideration C. manpower
D. maintenance E. commensurate

28. An understanding of the AIMS of an organization by the staff will AID greatly in increasing the DEMAND of the correspondence work of the office, and will to a large extent DETERMINE the NATURE of the correspondence. 28.____

A. aims B. aid C. demand
D. determine E. nature

29. BECAUSE the Civil Service Commission strongly feels that the MERIT system is a key factor in the MAINTENANCE of democratic government, it has adopted as one of its major DEFENSES the progressive democratization of its own PROCEDURES in dealing with candidates for positions in the public service. 29.____

A. Because B. merit C. maintenance
D. defenses E. procedures

30. Retirement and pensions systems are ESSENTIAL not only to provide employees with a means of support in the future, but also to prevent longevity and CHARITABLE considerations from UPSETTING the PROMOTIONAL opportunities for RETIRED members of the career service. 30.____

A. essential B. charitable C. upsetting
D. promotional E. retired

31. Suppose that the amount of money spent for supplies in 2005 for a division of a department was $15,650. This represented an increase of 12% over the amount spent for supplies for this division in 2004. The amount of money spent for supplies for this division in 2004 was MOST NEARLY 31.____

A. $13,973 B. $13,772 C. $14,346 D. $13,872

32. Suppose that a group of five clerks have been assigned to insert 24,000 letters into envelopes. The clerks perform this work at the following rates of speed: Clerk A, 1100 letters an hour; Clerk B, 1450 letters an hour; Clerk C, 1200 letters an hour; Clerk D, 1300 letters an hour; Clerk E, 1250 letters an hour. At the end of two hours of work, Clerks C and D are assigned to another task. Fron the time that Clerks C and D were taken off the assignment, the number of hours required for the remaining clerks to complete this assignment is 32.____

A. less than 3 hours
B. 3 hours
C. more than 3 hours, but less than 4 hours
D. more than 4 hours

33. The employees were SKEPTICAL about the usefulness of the new procedure. The word *skeptical,* as used in this sentence, means MOST NEARLY 33.____

A. enthusiastic
B. indifferent
C. doubtful
D. misinformed

34. He presented ABSTRUSE reasons in defense of his proposal. The word *abstruse,* as used in this sentence, means MOST NEARLY 34.____

A. unnecessary under the circumstances
B. apparently without merit or value
C. hard to be understood
D. obviously sound

35. A program of AUSTERITY is in effect in many countries. The word *austerity,* as used in this sentence, means MOST NEARLY 35.____

A. rigorous self-restraint
B. military censorship
C. rugged individualism
D. self-indulgence

36. The terms of the contract were ABROGATED at the last meeting of the board. The *word abrogated,* as used in this sentence, means MOST NEARLY 36.____

A. discussed
B. summarized
C. agreed upon
D. annulled

37. The enforcement of STRINGENT regulations is a difficult task. The word *stringent,* as used in this sentence, means MOST NEARLY 37.____

A. unreasonable
B. strict
C. unpopular
D. obscure

38. You should not DISPARAGE the value of his suggestions. The word *disparage,* as used in this sentence, means MOST NEARLY 38.____

A. ignore
B. exaggerate
C. belittle
D. reveal

39. The employee's conduct was considered REPREHENSIBLE by his superior. The word *reprehensible,* as used in this sentence, means MOST NEARLY 39.____

A. worthy of reward or honor
B. in accordance with rules and regulations
C. detrimental to efficiency and morale
D. deserving of censure or rebuke

40. He said he would EMULATE the persistence of his co-workers. The word *emulate*, as used in this sentence, means MOST NEARLY 40.____

A. strive to equal
B. acknowledge
C. encourage
D. attach no significance to

41. The revised regulations on discipline contained several MITIGATING provisions. The word *mitigating*, as used in this sentence, means MOST NEARLY 41.____

A. making more effective
B. containing contradictions
C. rendering less harsh
D. producing much criticism

42. The arrival of the inspector at the office on that day was FORTUITOUS. The word *fortuitous*, as used in this sentence, means MOST NEARLY 42.____

A. accidental
B. unfortunate
C. prearranged
D. desirable

43. A clerk who comes across the abbreviation *et.al.* should know that it stands for 43.____

A. for example
B. and others
C. disposition pending
D. and every month thereafter

Questions 44-50.

DIRECTIONS: Questions 44 through 50 are to be answered SOLELY on the basis of the following information.

Assume that the following regulations were established in your department to compute vacation allowances for services rendered by its employees during the period from June 1, 2007 through May 31, 2008. You are to determine the answer to each of the questions on the basis of these regulations.

VACATION REGULATIONS
(For the Period June 1, 2007 - May 31, 2008)

The vacation allowance for this period is to be taken after May 31, 2008.

Standard Vacation Allowance

Permanent per annum employees shall be granted 25 days vacation for a full year's service in such status. Employees who have served less than a full year in a permanent per annum status shall receive an allowance of 2 days for each month of such service.

Per diem employees shall be granted 1 1/2 days vacation for each month of service in such status.

Temporary employees shall be granted one day of vacation for each month of service in such status.

No vacation credit shall accrue to employees for the time they are on leave of absence.

Additional Allowance for Overtime

One day of vacation allowance shall be granted for each seven hours of accrued overtime. Where there is a balance of less than 7 hours of accrued overtime, one-half day of vacation shall be granted for each 3 1/2 hours of such overtime. In no case shall the additional vacation allowed for accrued overtime exceed 6 days.

Deductions for Excessive Sick Leave

Sick leave allowance for all employees, regardless of length of service, shall be 12 days for the year. Sick leave taken in excess of 12 days shall be deducted from vacation allowance. Any unused sick leave balance will be canceled on May 31, 2008.

Deductions for Excessive Lateness

Deductions for excessive lateness shall be made from vacation allowance in accordance with the following schedule:

No. of Times Late	Deduction from Vacation Allowance
0-50	no deduction
51-60	1/2 day
61-70	1 day
71-80	1 1/2 days
81-90	2 days
91-100	2 1/2 days
101-120	4 days
121-140	6 days
141 or over	penalty to be determined by Secretary of Department

Unused Vacation

Unused vacation allowance earned during the previous year shall be added to the current vacation allowance, up to a maximum of twelve days.

Note that the vacation allowances are for services rendered during the year ending May 31, 2008, and that computations for all employees are to be made as of that date.

44. Employee A served as a temporary employee from June 1, 2007 through January 31, 2008, and as a permanent per annum employee from February 1, 2008 through May 31, 2008. During the year, he accumulated 45 1/2 hours of overtime and was late 65 times. His vacation allowance should be ______ days. 44.____

A. 16 B. 15 C. 21 1/2 D. 21

45. Employee B was newly appointed to the department as a per diem employee on September 1, 2007. During the year, he took 15 days of sick leave and was late 48 times. His vacation allowance should be ______ days. 45.____

A. less than 10
B. 10 1/2
C. 15
D. 12 1/2

46. Employee C has been a permanent per annum employee throughout the year. He had 15 days of vacation due him from the previous year. During the year, he was late 85 times, he took 10 days of sick leave, and he accumulated 38 1/2 hours of overtime. His vacation allowance should be _______ days. 46.____

A. 38 1/2
B. 42 1/2
C. 40 1/2
D. more than 43

47. Employee D was newly appointed to the department as a permanent per annum employee on July 1, 2007. He was on leave of absence from December 1, 2007 through February 28, 2008. During the year, he took 6 days of sick leave, he was late 70 times, and he accumulated 21 hours of overtime. His vacation allowance should be _______ days. 47.____

A. 24
B. 18
C. 17 1/2
D. 19 1/2

48. Employee E served as a per diem employee from June 1, 2007 through July 31, 2007, and as a permanent per annum employee from August 1, 2007 to May 31, 2008. He had 6 days of vacation due him from the previous year. During the year, he took 13 days of sick leave, he accumulated 70 hours of overtime, and he was late 132 times. His vacation allowance should be _______ days. 48.____

A. less than 29
B. 29
C. 30
D. more than 30

49. The maximum total vacation allowance which a permanent per annum employee can have due him by May 31, 2008 is _______ days. 49.____

A. 43
B. 25
C. 31
D. 37

50. An employee who has served as a temporary employee for 6 months and as a permanent per annum employee for 6 months will earn exactly 50.____

A. two-thirds as much vacation as an employee who has been on a permanent per annum basis for the whole year
B. as much vacation as an employee who has been on a per diem basis for the whole year
C. as much vacation as an employee who has been on a per diem basis for 4 months and on a permanent per annum basis for 8 months
D. as much vacation as an employee who has been on a per diem basis for 8 months and on a permanent per annum basis for 5 months

Questions 51-60.

DIRECTIONS: Each of Questions 51 through 60 may be classified under one of the following four categories:

A. faulty because of incorrect grammar or sentence structure
B. faulty because of incorrect punctuation
C. faulty because of incorrect spelling
D. correct

Examine each sentence carefully to determine under which of the above four options it is best classified. Then, in the space at the right, write the letter preceding the option which is the BEST of the four suggested above. Each incorrect sentence contains but one type of error. Consider a sentence to be correct if it contains none of the types of errors mentioned, even though there may be other correct ways of expressing the same thought.

51. Although the department's supply of scratch pads and stationery have diminished considerably, the allotment for our division has not been reduced. 51.____

52. You have not told us whom you wish to designate as your secretary. 52.____

53. Upon reading the minutes of the last meeting, the new proposal was taken up for consideration. 53.____

54. Before beginning the discussion, we locked the door as a precautionery measure. 54.____

55. The supervisor remarked, "Only those clerks, who perform routine work, are permitted to take a rest period." 55.____

56. Not only will this duplicating machine make accurate copies, but it will also produce a quantity of work equal to fifteen transcribing typists. 56.____

57. "Mr. Jones," said the supervisor, "we regret our inability to grant you an extention of your leave of absence." 57.____

58. Although the employees find the work monotonous and fatigueing, they rarely complain. 58.____

59. We completed the tabulation of the receipts on time despite the fact that Miss Smith our fastest operator was absent for over a week. 59.____

60. The reaction of the employees who attended the meeting, as well as the reaction of those who did not attend, indicates clearly that the schedule is satisfactory to everyone concerned. 60.____

KEY (CORRECT ANSWERS)

1.	C	16.	D	31.	A	46.	C
2.	D	17.	B	32.	B	47.	B
3.	D	18.	B	33.	C	48.	A
4.	B	19.	A	34.	C	49.	A
5.	A	20.	D	35.	A	50.	B
6.	A	21.	C	36.	D	51.	A
7.	C	22.	B	37.	B	52.	D
8.	C	23.	D	38.	C	53.	A
9.	B	24.	C	39.	D	54.	C
10.	C	25.	A	40.	A	55.	B
11.	D	26.	E	41.	C	56.	A
12.	C	27.	A	42.	A	57.	C
13.	C	28.	C	43.	B	58.	C
14.	B	29.	D	44.	D	59.	B
15.	D	30.	E	45.	B	60.	D

EXAMINATION SECTION
TEST 1

DIRECTIONS: Each question or incomplete statement is followed by several suggested answers or completions. Select the one that BEST answers the question or completes the statement. *PRINT THE LETTER OF THE CORRECT ANSWER IN THE SPACE AT THE RIGHT.*

1. As the supervisor of a staff of clerical employees performing various types of work, you are responsible for the accuracy and efficiency with which their work is performed. Of the following actions you may take to insure the accuracy of their work, the MOST practical one is for you to 1.____

   A. review each operation completed by a staff member before permitting the employee to proceed to the next operation
   B. keep a record of every error made by an employee and use this record to determine whether a careless employee should be transferred or discharged
   C. assign work in such a way that every operation is performed independently by two employees
   D. determine what errors are likely to occur and set up safeguards to prevent the occurrence of these errors

2. Assume that you are the supervisor of a small clerical unit. One of your subordinates has violated a staff regulation by failing to inform you that he will be absent on a certain day. Of the following, the MOST appropriate action for you to take first is to 2.____

   A. discuss this matter with your immediate superior
   B. find out the reason for his failure to obey this staff regulation
   C. determine what disciplinary action other supervisors have taken in similar cases
   D. take no action if his absence did not interfere with the work of the unit; reprimand him if it did

3. A newly appointed clerk is assigned to a unit of an agency at a time when the supervisor of the unit is very busy and has little time to devote to instructing the new employee in the work he is to perform. Of the following, the MOST appropriate method of training this employee is for the supervisor to 3.____

   A. instruct the new employee to observe several experienced clerks at work and question them regarding any aspect of the work he does not understand
   B. delegate the job of training this employee to an employee in the unit who is qualified to instruct him
   C. assign the new employee a simple task and inform him that more complex and varied duties will be given him when the supervisor is less busy
   D. have the employee spend his time reading the agency's annual reports and the laws, rules, and regulations governing its work

4. As a supervisor, you may find it necessary to consult with your superior before taking action on some matters. Of the following, the action for which it is MOST important that you obtain the prior approval of your superior is one that involves 4.____

A. assuming additional functions for your unit
B. rotating assignments among your staff members
C. initiating regular meetings of your staff
D. assigning certain members of your staff to work overtime on an emergency job

5. Suppose that a clerk who is employed in a unit under your supervision performs his work quickly but carelessly. He is about to be transferred to another unit in your department. The chief of this other unit asks you for your opinion of this employee's work habits. Of the following, the MOST appropriate reply for you to make is to 5.____

A. point out this employee's good qualities only since he may correct his bad qualities after his transfer is effected
B. say nothing good or bad about this employee, thus permitting him to start his new assignment with a clean slate
C. inform the unit chief that this clerk performed his work speedily but was careless
D. emphasize this employee's good points and minimize his bad points

6. When subordinates request his advice in solving problems encountered in their work, a certain bureau chief occasionally answers the request by first asking the subordinate what he thinks should be done. This action by the bureau chief is, on the whole, 6.____

A. *desirable* because it stimulates subordinates to give more thought to the solution of problems encountered
B. *undesirable* because it discourages subordinates from asking questions
C. *desirable* because it discourages subordinates from asking questions
D. *undesirable* because it undermines the confidence of subordinates in the ability of their supervisor

7. Of the following factors that may be considered by a unit head in dealing with the tardy subordinate, the one which should be given LEAST consideration is the 7.____

A. frequency with which the employee is tardy
B. effect of the employee's tardiness upon the work of other employees
C. willingness of the employee to work overtime when necessary
D. cause of the employee's tardiness

8. Of the following, the action that is likely to contribute MOST to the prestige of a supervisor is for him to 8.____

A. expect all his subordinates to perform with equal efficiency any tasks assigned to them
B. observe the same rules of conduct that he expects his subordinates to observe
C. seek their advice on his personal problems and offer them his advice on their personal problems
D. be always frank and outspoken to his subordinates in pointing out their faults

9. Although an employee under your supervision frequently protests when receiving a monotonous assignment, he nevertheless performs the assigned task efficiently. His protests, however, disturb the other employees and interfere with their work. Of the following actions you may take in handling this employee, the MOST desirable one is for you to 9.____

A. point out to him the effect of his conduct on the staff's work and request his cooperation in accepting such assignments
B. arrange to issue such assignments to him when the other members of his staff are not present
C. inform him that you will request his transfer to another unit unless he puts a halt to his unjustifiable protests
D. ask other members of the staff to tell him that he is disturbing them by his protests

10. Assume that you are the supervisor of a small clerical unit which tabulates data prepared by another unit. One of your employees calls your attention to what appears to be an erroneous figure. 10.____
Of the following, the MOST acceptable advice for you to give this employee is to tell him to

A. omit the figure containing the apparent error and continue with the tabulation
B. make whatever change in the erroneous figure that appears warranted and notify the supervisor of the unit which prepared the data that errors are being made by his staff
C. accept the questionable figure as correct and continue with the tabulation since there is no certainty that an error has been made
D. ask the supervisor of the unit that prepared the data to have the questionable figure checked for accuracy and corrected if it is erroneous

11. A clerk in an agency informs Mr. Brown, an applicant for a license issued by the agency, that the application filed by him was denied because he lacks a year and six months of required experience. Shortly after the applicant leaves the agency's office, the clerk realizes that Mr. Brown lacks only six months of required experience rather than a year and six months. 11.____
Of the following, the MOST desirable procedure to be followed in connection with this matter is that

A. a printed copy of the requirements should be sent to Mr. Brown
B. a letter explaining and correcting the error should be sent to Mr. Brown
C. no action should be taken because Mr. Brown is not qualified at the present time for the license
D. a report of this matter should be prepared and attached to Mr. Brown's application for reference if Mr. Brown should file another application

12. Mr. Stone, who has been recently placed in charge of a clerical unit staffed with ten employees, plans to institute several radical changes in the procedures of his unit. 12.____
Of the following actions he may take before adopting any of the revisions, the MOST desirable one is for Mr. Stone to

A. distribute to each staff member a memorandum describing the revised procedures and requesting the staff's cooperation in giving the revised procedures a fair trial
B. issue to each staff member a memorandum describing the proposed changes and inviting him to submit his written criticism of these proposed changes
C. issue to each staff member a memorandum describing the proposed changes and notifying him of the time and date of a staff conference to be held on the merits of the proposed changes
D. discuss the proposed changes with each staff member independently and obtain his opinion of the proposed changes

13. An assignment completed by Frank King is returned to him by his unit supervisor for certain changes. Frank King objects to making these changes. 13.____
Of the following, the MOST appropriate action for the unit supervisor to take first is to

A. permit Frank King to present his arguments against making these changes
B. inform Frank King that he is free to take the matter up with a higher authority
C. reprimand Frank King for objecting and assign another employee to make these changes
D. state briefly that his decision is final and indicate by his manner that further discussion would be useless

14. A properly conducted job analysis will reveal the qualities essential for efficient job performance. 14.____
Of the following, the MOST accurate implication of this statement is that job analysis

A. enables the supervisor to standardize procedures
B. aids the supervisor in fitting the man to the job
C. is helpful to the supervisor in scheduling work
D. assists the supervisor in estimating costs of jobs

15. All of us who are employed by a government agency are, figuratively speaking, living in glass houses. 15.____
Of the following, this quotation MOST nearly means that employees of government agencies are

A. basically secure in their positions
B. more closely supervised than are those in private industry
C. not free to exercise initiative
D. subject to constant surveillance

16. So important to good supervision is effective leadership that some supervisors who are well equipped in this respect have compensated for deficiencies in other supervisory qualities. 16.____
On the basis of this statement, the MOST accurate of the following statements is that

A. supervisory ability is the most valuable attribute a leader can have
B. effective leaders are generally deficient in other supervisory qualities
C. other supervisory qualities may be substituted for leadership ability
D. good leaders may make good supervisors even though lacking in other supervisory qualities

17. The improvement in skill and the development of proper attitudes are essential factors in the building of correct work habits. 17.____
Of the following, the MOST valid implication of this statement for a supervisor is that

A. the more skilled an employee is, the better will be his attitude toward his work
B. developing proper attitudes in subordinates toward their work is more time-consuming for the supervisor than improving their skill
C. the improvement of a worker's skill is only part of a supervisor's job
D. correct work habits are established in order to either improve the skill of workers or develop in them a proper attitude toward their work

Questions 18-21.

DIRECTIONS: Questions 18 through 21 are based upon the situation described below. Consider the facts given in this situation when answering these questions.

SITUATION: You are the supervisor of a small unit in a large department. In order to assist your staff in handling a peak work load, ten temporary clerks have been hired for a period of two months.

18. Of the following actions you may take before assigning specific tasks to these temporary employees, the MOST appropriate action is for you to 18.____

    A. designate one of their number as your supervisory assistant
    B. find out what clerical experience and training each one has had
    C. ask each member of this group to indicate the type of work he prefers to do
    D. escort this group throughout the department, introducing each temporary employee to all the unit heads in the department

19. The ten temporary employees have been grouped into two teams of five employees each, and the two teams have been given different assignments. After working with his group for several days, an employee in one group asks to be transferred to the other group. 19.____
    Of the following reasons for transferring this employee to the other group, the LEAST acceptable one is that

    A. there is a clash in temperament between him and some of the other members of his group
    B. he can perform the work assigned to the other group more efficiently than he can perform the work assigned to his group
    C. the work assigned to the other group is less monotonous than that assigned to his group
    D. the work assigned to his present group compels him to take frequent rest periods because of a physical disability

20. One of the temporary employees informs you that he has a suggestion for improving the method of performing the work assigned to his group. 20.____
    Of the following actions, the MOST desirable one for you to take is to

    A. ignore his suggestion since he knows little about the purpose of the assignment
    B. ask him to try out the suggestion before submitting it to you
    C. have him discuss it with his co-workers before submitting it to you
    D. listen to his suggestion and take appropriate action

21. A temporary clerk who had been decreasing the amount of work he performed and who had also been attempting to induce other temporary clerks to reduce their production was twice cautioned by you to cease these practices. On each occasion, he promised to discontinue these improper practices and to perform his work conscientiously and cooperatively. Soon thereafter, he is detected for the third time attempting to persuade the other temporary clerks to shirk their duties. 21.____
    Of the following, the MOST appropriate action for you to take is to

A. reprimand him for his improper conduct and have him transferred immediately to another unit
B. remind him that he may not be employed again as a temporary clerk if he continues his unethical practices
C. call a meeting of the temporary staff and warn them that anyone whose production falls below average will be discharged
D. report his improper practices to your immediate superior and recommend that this employee's services be terminated

22. As a supervisor in an agency, you receive a letter from the head of a civic organization requesting information which you are not permitted to divulge. 22.____
In preparing your letter of reply, it is MOST desirable that you

A. begin with a pleasant phrase or statement and conclude with a brief statement denying the request
B. limit your reply to a brief statement denying the request
C. place the denial of the request between a pleasant opening phrase or statement and a cordial closing statement
D. begin with a denial of the request and conclude with a pleasant closing statement

23. Of the following, it is LEAST essential for a supervisor, in assigning work to a subordinate, to issue written instructions when the 23.____

A. supervisor will be on hand to check the work
B. instructions are to be passed on to other employees
C. assignment involves many details
D. subordinate is to be held strictly accountable for the work performed

24. The suggestion is made that all the secretaries assigned to the bureau chiefs of a certain agency can be transferred to a newly established central transcribing unit which is to be staffed with stenographers and typists. Of the following, the MOST probable effect of reassigning these secretaries would be that 24.____

A. the quality of the stenographic and typing work performed by the secretaries would deteriorate
B. the bureau chiefs would be burdened with much of the routine work that is now performed by their secretaries
C. typing and stenographic work would be performed less expeditiously and with frequent delays
D. the development of understudies for bureau chiefs would be greatly hampered

25. In a large agency where both men and women are employed as clerks, certain duties may be assigned more appropriately to women than to men. 25.____
Of the following, the assignment that is generally MOST appropriate for a woman clerk is

A. sorting and filing 3x5 index cards
B. issuing supplies from the agency's stockroom to employees presenting requisitions
C. serving at an information desk during the hours from 7:00 P.M. to 11:00 P.M. for a period of two months
D. collecting outgoing mail from the various offices of the agency and delivering incoming mail to these offices

26. A unit supervisor discovers several errors in the work performed by a subordinate. In dealing with this subordinate, it is LEAST desirable for the supervisor to 26.____

A. give his criticism immediately rather than at a later date
B. make it clear to the subordinate that he is criticizing the subordinate and not the subordinate's work
C. praise, when possible, some commendable aspect of the subordinate's work before making the adverse criticism
D. make sure that his criticism is not overheard by other employees

27. The status of the morale of a staff is usually a good indication of the quality of the leadership displayed by the supervisor of the staff. 27.____
Of the following, the BEST indication of the existence of high morale among a staff is that

A. the employees are prompt in reporting for work
B. the staff is always willing to subordinate personal desires to attain group objectives
C. it is seldom necessary for the staff to work overtime
D. the subordinates and their superior meet socially after working hours

28. The use of standard practices and procedures in large organizations is often essential in order to insure a smooth, efficient, and controlled flow of work. A strict adherence to standard practices and procedures to the extent that unnecessary delay is created is known, in general, as *red tape.* 28.____
On the basis of this statement, the MOST accurate of the following statements is that

A. although the use of standard practices and procedures promotes efficiency, it also creates unnecessary delays and *red tape*
B. in order to insure a smooth, efficient, and controlled plan of work, *red tape* should be eliminated by a strict adherence to standard practices and procedures
C. *red tape* is a necessary evil which invariably creeps into any large organization which uses standard practices and procedures
D. *red* tape exists when delay takes place as a result of a too rigid conformity with standard practices and procedures

29. The tasks of government are imposed not only by law but also by public opinion, which at any time may be made into law. Government agencies must, therefore, strive to anticipate and fulfill the needs of the public. 29.____
Of the following, the MOST valid implication of this statement is that the

A. satisfaction of the needs of the public is one of the obligations of a government agency
B. law prescribes what tasks government agencies should perform and public opinion determines how these tasks should be performed
C. tasks imposed by law on a government agency have priority over those imposed by public opinion
D. functions of a government agency should be carried out in accordance with the letter, rather than the spirit, of the law

30. The manner in which an employee performs on the job rather than his potential ability is the true test of his value to his employer. 30.____
The one of the following which is NOT an implication of the above statement is a(n)

A. employee of great potential ability may be of little or no value to his employer
B. supervisor should observe the manner in which his subordinates perform their work
C. employee's potential ability is of no significance in determining his fitness for a specific job
D. employee should attempt to perform his work to the best of his ability

31. No routine will automatically bring itself into proper relation with changing conditions. Of the following situations, the one which MOST NEARLY exemplifies the truth of this statement is a 31.____

A. change in the rules governing the submission or reports by employees working in the field is found to be impractical and the previous procedure is reinstituted
B. long established method of filing papers in a bureau is found to be inadequate because of changes in the functions of the bureau
C. long established method of distributing orders to the staff is found to work effectively when the size of the staff is considerably increased
D. change in the rules governing hours of attendance at work proves distasteful to many employees

32. Interest is essentially an attitude of continuing attentiveness, found where activity is satisfactorily self-expressive. Whenever work is so circumscribed that the chance for self-expression or development is denied, monotony is present. 32.____
On the basis of this statement, it is MOST accurate to state that

A. tasks which are repetitive in nature do not permit self-expression and, therefore, create monotony
B. interest in one's work is increased by financial and non-financial incentives
C. jobs which are monotonous can be made self-expressive by substituting satisfactory working conditions
D. workers whose tasks afford them no opportunity for self-expression find such tasks to be monotonous

33. The first step in an organizational study is the reading of the basic documents. There is some documentary basis for any governmental organization, outlining the purposes for which it was established, conferring certain powers, and imposing certain limitations on the conferred powers. This statement indicates that in making an organization study, one should FIRST 33.____

A. review all the authoritative material in the field of government administration and organization
B. arrange the functions of the organization on a functional chart in accordance with the official documents
C. study the laws and authorities under which the organization operates
D. outline the purposes for which the organization study was originally established

34. His attitude is as provincial as an isolationist country's unwillingness to engage in any international trade whatever, on the ground that it will be required to buy something from outsiders which could possibly be produced by local talent, although not as well and not as cheaply. This statement is MOST descriptive of the attitude of the division chief in a government agency who 34.____

A. wishes to restrict promotions to supervisory positions in his division exclusively to employees in his division
B. refuses to delegate responsible tasks to subordinates qualified to perform these tasks
C. believes that informal on-the-job training of new staff members is superior to formal training methods
D. frequently makes personal issues out of matters that should be handled on an impersonal basis

35. A trainee was paid a weekly wage of $480.00 for a 40-hour work week. As a result of a new labor contract, he is paid $494.00 a week for a 38-hour work week with time-and-one-half pay for time worked in excess of 38 hours in any work week. 35.____
If he continues to work 40 hours weekly under the new contract, the amount by which his average hourly rate for a 40-hour work week under the new contract exceeds the hourly rate previously paid him lies between ______ and ______, inclusive.

A. $1.02; $1.06 B. $1.08; $1.16 C. $1.18; $1.26 D. $1.28; $1.36

36. The problem of inadequate storage space arising from the large number of inactive records stored in city agencies can be solved MOST satisfactorily with the aid of ______ equipment. 36.____

A. photostat
B. microfilm
C. IBM sorting
D. digital printing

37. To say that an employee is *erudite* means MOST NEARLY that he is 37.____

A. scholarly
B. insecure
C. efficient
D. punctual

38. The forms design section of a city agency recommended that the sizes of forms used by the agency be limited to the sizes that can be cut with the least amount of waste from either 17" x 22" or 17" x 28" sheets. 38.____
Of the following, the size that does NOT comply with this recommendation is

A. 4 1/2" x 5 1/2"
B. 3 3/4" x 4 1/4"
C. 3 1/2" x 4 1/4"
D. 4 1/4" x 2 3/4"

39. The number of investigations conducted by an agency in 2007 was 3,600. In 2008, the number of investigations conducted was one-third more than in 2007. The number of investigations conducted in 2009 was three-fourths of the number conducted in 2008. It is anticipated that the number of investigations conducted in 2010 will be equal to the average of the three preceding years. 39.____
On the basis of this information, the MOST accurate of the following statements is that the number of investigations conducted in

A. 2007 is larger than the number anticipated for 2010
B. 2008 is smaller than the number anticipated for 2010
C. 2009 is equal to the number conducted in 2007
D. 2009 is larger than the number anticipated for 2010

40. *The office manager thought it advisable to MOLLIFY his subordinate.* The word *mollify* as used in this sentence means MOST NEARLY 40.___

A. reprimand B. caution C. calm D. question

41. *The bureau chief adopted a DILATORY policy.* The word *dilatory* as used in this sentence means MOST NEARLY 41.___

A. tending to cause delay
B. acceptable to all affected
C. severe but fair
D. prepared with great care

42. *He complained about the PAUCITY of requests.* The word *paucity* as used in this sentence means MOST NEARLY 42.___

A. great variety
B. unreasonableness
C. unexpected increase
D. scarcity

43. To say that an event is *imminent* means MOST NEARLY that it is 43.___

A. near at hand
B. unpredictable
C. favorable or happy
D. very significant

44. *The general manager delivered a LAUDATORY speech.* The word *laudatory* as used in this sentence means MOST NEARLY 44.___

A. clear and emphatic
B. lengthy
C. introductory
D. expressing praise

45. *We all knew of his AVERSION for performing statistical work.* The word *aversion* as used in this sentence means MOST NEARLY 45.___

A. training
B. dislike
C. incentive
D. lack of preparation

46. *The engineer was CIRCUMSPECT in making his recommendations.* The word *circumspect* as used in this sentence means MOST NEARLY 46.___

A. hostile B. outspoken C. biased D. cautious

47. To say that certain clerical operations were *obviated* means MOST NEARLY that these operations were 47.___

A. extremely distasteful
B. easily understood
C. made unnecessary
D. very complicated

48. *The interviewer was impressed with the client's DEMEANOR.* The word *demeanor* as used in this sentence means MOST NEARLY 48.___

A. outward manner
B. plan of action
C. fluent speech
D. extensive knowledge

49. To say that the information was *gratuitous* means MOST NEARLY that it was 49.___

A. given freely
B. deeply appreciated
C. brief
D. valuable

50. *The supervisor was unaware of this EXIGENCY.* The word *exigency* as used in this sentence means MOST NEARLY 50.___

A. unexplained absence
B. costly delay
C. pressing need
D. final action

51. *She considered the supervisor's action to be ARBITRARY.* The word *arbitrary* as used in this sentence means MOST NEARLY 51.____

A. inconsistent
B. justifiable
C. appeasing
D. dictatorial

52. *His report on the activities of the agency was VERBOSE.* The word *verbose* as used in this sentence means MOST NEARLY 52.____

A. vivid B. wordy C. vague D. oral

Questions 53-61.

DIRECTIONS: Questions 53 through 61 are to be answered SOLELY on the basis of the following information.

Assume that the following rules for computing service ratings are to be used experimentally in determining the service ratings of seven permanent employees. (Note that these rules are hypothetical and are NOT to be confused with the existing method of computing service ratings for employees.) The personnel record of each of these seven employees is given in Table II. You are to determine the answer to each of the questions on the basis of the rules given below for computing service ratings and the data contained in the personnel records of these seven employees.

All computations should be made as of the close of the rating period ending March 31, 2007.

<u>*RULES FOR COMPUTING SERVICE RATINGS*</u>

<u>*Service Rating*</u>
The service rating of each permanent competitive class employee shall be computed by adding the following three scores: (1) a basic score, (2) the employee's seniority score, and (3) the employee's efficiency score.

<u>*Seniority Score*</u>
An employee's seniority score shall be computed by crediting him with 1/2% per year for each year of service starting with the date of the employee's entrance as a permanent employee into the competitive class, up to a maximum of 15 years (7 1/2%). A residual fractional period of eight months or more shall be considered as a full year and credited with 1/2%. A residual fraction of from four to, but not including, eight months shall be considered as a half-year and credited with 1/4%. A residual fraction of less than four months shall receive no credit in the seniority score. For example, a person who entered the competitive class as a permanent employee on August 1, 1999 would, as of March 31, 2002, be credited with a seniority score of 1 1/2% for his two years and 8 months of service.

<u>*Efficiency Score*</u>
An employee's efficiency score shall be computed by adding the annual efficiency ratings received by him during his service in his PRESENT position. (Where there are negative efficiency ratings, such ratings shall be subtracted from the sum of the positive efficiency ratings.) An employee's annual efficiency rating shall be based on the grade he receives from his supervisor for his work performance during the annual efficiency rating period.

Basic Score

A basic score of 70% shall be given to each employee upon permanent appointment to a competitive class position.

An employee shall receive a grade of "A" for performing work of the highest quality and shall be credited with an efficiency rating of plus (+) 3%, An employee shall receive a grade of "F" for performing work of the lowest quality and shall receive an efficiency rating of minus (-) 2%. Table I, entitled "Basis for Determining Annual Efficiency Ratings," lists the six grades of work performance with their equivalent annual efficiency ratings. Table I also lists the efficiency ratings to be assigned for service in a position for less than a year during the annual efficiency rating period. The annual efficiency rating period shall run from April 1 to March 31, inclusive.

TABLE I

BASIS FOE DETERMINING ANNUAL EFFICIENCY RATINGS

		Annual Efficiency Rating for Service in a Position for:		
Quality of Work Performed	Grade Assigned A	8 months to a full year	At least 4 months but less than 8 months	Less than 4 months
Highest Quality	A	+ 3%	+1½%	0%
Good Quality	B	+ 2%	+ 1%	0%
Standard Quality	C	+ 1%	+½%	0%
Substandard Quality	D	0%	0%	0%
Poor Quality	E	-1%	-½%	0%
Lowest Quality	F	-2%	-1%	0%

Appointment or Promotion during an Efficiency Rating Period

An employee who has been appointed or promoted during an efficiency rating period shall receive for that period an efficiency rating only for work performed by him during the portion of the period that he served in the position to which he was appointed or promoted. His efficiency rating for the period shall be determined in accordance with Table I.

Sample Computation of Service Rating

John Smith entered the competitive class as a permanent employee on December 1, 2002 and was promoted to his present position as a Clerk, Grade 3 on November 1, 2005. As a Clerk, Grade 3, he received a grade of "B" for work performed during the five-month period extending from November 1, 2005 to March 31, 2006 and a grade of "C" for work performed during the full annual period extending from April 1, 2006 to March 32, 2007.

On the basis of the Rules for Computing Service Ratings, John Smith should be credited with:

70 % basic score
2 1/4% seniority score - for 4 years and 4 months of service (from 12-1-02 to 3-31-07)
2 % efficiency score - for 5 months of "B" service and a full year of "C" service
74 1/4%

TABLE II

PERSONNEL RECORD OF SEVEN PERMANENT COMPETITIVE CLASS EMPLOYEES

Employee	*Present Position*	*Date of Appointment or Promotion to Present Position*	*Date of Entry as Permanent Employee in Competitive Class*
Allen	*Clerk, Gr. 5*	*6-1-03*	*7-1-90*
Brown	*Clerk, Gr. 4*	*1-1-05*	*7-1-97*
Cole	*Clerk, Gr. 3*	*9-1-03*	*11-1-00*
Fox	*Clerk, Gr. 3*	*10-1-03*	*9-1-98*
Green	*Clerk, Gr. 2*	*12-1-01*	*12-1-01*
Hunt	*Clerk, Gr. 2*	*7-1-02*	*7-1-02*
Kane	*Steno, Gr. 3*	*11-16-04*	*3-1-01*

	Grades Received Annually for Work Performed in Present Position					
Employee	*4-1-01 to 3-31-02*	*4-1-02 to 3-31-03*	*4-1-03 to 3-31-04*	*4-1-04 to 3-31-05*	*4-1-05 to 3-31-06*	*4-1- -06 to 3-31 -07*
Allen			*C **	*C*	*B*	*C*
Brown				*C**	*C*	*B*
Cole			*A**	*B*	*C*	*C*
Fox			*C**	*C*	*D*	*C*
Green	*C**	*D*	*C*	*D*	*C*	*C*
Hunt		*C**	*C*	*E*	*C*	*C*
Kane				*B**	*B*	*C*

Explanatory Notes:

** Served in present position for less than a full year during this rating period. (Note date of appointment, or promotion, to present period.)*

All seven employees have served continuously as permanent employees since their entry into the competitive class.

Questions 53 through 61 refer to the employees listed in Table II. You are to answer these questions SOLELY on the basis of the preceding Rules for Computing Service Ratings and on the information concerning these seven employees given in Table II. You are reminded that all computations are to be made as of the close of the rating period ending March 31, 2007. Candidates may find it helpful to arrange their computations on their scratch paper in an orderly manner since the computations for one question may also be utilized in answering another question.

53. The seniority score of Allen is 53.___

A. 74% B. 8 1/2% C. 8% D. 8 1/4%

54. The seniority score of Fox exceeds that of Cole by 54.___

A. 1 1/2% B. 2% C. 1% D. 3/4 1/4

55. The seniority score of Brown is 55.___

A. equal to Hunt's
B. twice Hunt's
C. more than Hunt's by 1 1/2%
D. less than Hunt's by 1/2%

56. Green's efficiency score is 56.___

A. twice that of Kane
B. equal to that of Kane
C. less than Kane's by 1/2%
D. less than Kane's by 1%

57. Of the following employees, the one who has the LOWEST efficiency score is 57.___

A. Brown B. Fox C. Hunt D. Kane

58. A comparison of Hunt's efficiency score with his seniority score reveals that his efficiency score is 58.___

A. less than his seniority score by 1/2%
B. less than his seniority score by 3/4%
C. equal to his seniority score
D. greater than his seniority score by 1/2%

59. Fox's service rating is 59.___

A. 72 1/2% B. 74% C. 76 1/2% D. 76 3/4%

60. Brown's service rating is 60.___

A. less than 78%
B. 78%
C. 78 1/4%
D. more than 78 1/4%

61. Cole's service rating exceeds Kane's by 61.___

A. less than 2%
B. 2%
C. 2 1/4%
D. more than 2 1/4%

Questions 62-71.

DIRECTIONS: Each of the sentences numbered 62 to 71 may be classified under one of the following four options:
(A) faulty; contains an error in grammar only
(B) faulty; contains an error in spelling only
(C) faulty; contains an error in grammar and an error in spelling
(D) correct; contains no error in grammar or in spelling

Examine each sentence carefully to determine under which of the above four options it is best classified. Then, in the correspondingly numbered space at the right, write the letter preceding the option which is the BEST of the four listed above.

62. A recognized principle of good management is that an assignment should be given to whomever is best qualified to carry it out. 62.____

63. He considered it a privilege to be allowed to review and summarize the technical reports issued annually by your agency. 63.____

64. Because the warehouse was in an inaccessable location, deliveries of electric fixtures from the warehouse were made only in large lots. 64.____

65. Having requisitioned the office supplies, Miss Brown returned to her desk and resumed the computation of petty cash disbursements. 65.____

66. One of the advantages of this chemical solution is that records treated with it are not inflammable. 66.____

67. The complaint of this employee, in addition to the complaints of the other employees, were submitted to the grievance committee. 67.____

68. A study of the duties and responsibilities of each of the various categories of employees was conducted by an unprejudiced classification analyst. 68.____

69. Ties of friendship with this subordinate compels him to withold the censure that the subordinate deserves. 69.____

70. Neither of the agencies are affected by the decision to institute a program for rehabilitating physically handicaped men and women. 70.____

71. The chairman stated that the argument between you and he was creating an intolerable situation. 71.____

Questions 72-75.

DIRECTIONS: Each of Questions 72 through 75 consists of a statement containing five words in capital letters. One of these capitalized words is not in keeping with the meaning which the statement is evidently intended to convey. The five words in capital letters in each statement are reprinted after the statement. In the correspondingly numbered space at the right, write the letter preceding the one of the five words which does MOST to spoil the true meaning of the statement.

72. The alert employee will find, EVEN in the best managed offices, violations of some of the rules of good office management. However, further study will reveal that the correction of such violations is by ALL means a SIMPLE matter, BUT requires research, time, patience, and often a high degree of MANAGERIAL ability. 72.____

A. Even B. All C. Simple D. But E. Managerial

73. The information clerk in any organization must DELEGATE tact, courtesy, and good judgment in DEALING with callers, many of whom, on the other hand, DISREGARD business ETIQUETTE in their CONTACT with the information clerk. 73.____

A. Delegate
B. Dealing
C. Disregard
D. Etiquette
E. Contact

74. When the supervisor gives advancement or other rewards only to SUBORDINATES who have REQUESTED them, or shows a sincere INTEREST in the welfare of his staff, he is building FAVORABLE ATTITUDES. 74.____

A. Subordinates
B. Requested
C. Interest
D. Favorable
E. Attitudes

75. An appointee to the City's civil service must be a bona fide resident of the City for at least three years immediately prior to his APPOINTMENT. An appointee who served in the Armed Forces retains as his legal address that place where he resided prior to his ENTRY into the MILITARY service, PROVIDED he has taken definite action to establish a new RESIDENCE. 75.____

A. Appointment
B. Entry
C. Military
D. Provided
E. Residence

KEY (CORRECT ANSWERS)

1.	D	16.	D	31.	B	46.	D	61.	A
2.	B	17.	C	32.	D	47.	C	62.	A
3.	B	18.	B	33.	C	48.	A	63.	D
4.	A	19.	C	34.	A	49.	A	64.	B
5.	C	20.	D	35.	D	50.	C	65.	D
6.	A	21.	D	36.	B	51.	D	66.	B
7.	C	22.	C	37.	A	52.	B	67.	A
8.	B	23.	A	38.	B	53.	A	68.	D
9.	A	24.	B	39.	C	54.	C	69.	C
10.	D	25.	A	40.	C	55.	B	70.	C
11.	B	26.	B	41.	A	56.	C	71.	A
12.	C	27.	B	42.	D	57.	B	72.	B
13.	A	28.	D	43.	A	58.	D	73.	A
14.	B	29.	A	44.	D	59.	D	74.	B
15.	D	30.	C	45.	B	60.	B	75.	D

READING COMPREHENSION
UNDERSTANDING AND INTERPRETING WRITTEN MATERIAL

EXAMINATION SECTION

TEST 1

DIRECTIONS: Each question or incomplete statement is followed by several suggested answers or completions. Select the one that BEST answers the question or completes the statement. *PRINT THE LETTER OF THE CORRECT ANSWER IN THE SPACE AT THE RIGHT.*

Questions 1-6.

DIRECTIONS: Questions 1 through 6 are to be answered SOLELY on the basis of the information contained in the following passage.

Duplicating is the process of making a number of identical copies of letters, documents, etc. from an original. Some duplicating processes make copies directly from the original document. Other duplicating processes require the preparation of a special master, and copies are then made from the master. Four of the most common duplicating processes are stencil, fluid, offset, and xerox.

In the stencil process, the typewriter is used to cut the words into a master called a stencil. Drawings, charts, or graphs can be cut into the stencil using a stylus. As many as 3,500 good-quality copies can be reproduced from one stencil. Various grades of finished paper from inexpensive mimeograph to expensive bond can be used.

The fluid process is a good method of copying from 50 to 125 good-quality copies from a master, which is prepared with a special dye. The master is placed on the duplicator, and special paper with a hard finish is moistened and then passed through the duplicator. Some of the dye on the master is dissolved, creating an impression on the paper. The impression becomes lighter as more copies are made; and once the dye on the master is used up, a new master must be made.

The offset process is the most adaptable office duplicating process because this process can be used for making a few copies or many copies. Masters can be made on paper or plastic for a few hundred copies, or on metal plates for as many as 75,000 copies. By using a special technique called photo-offset, charts, photographs, illustrations, or graphs can be reproduced on the master plate. The offset process is capable of producing large quantities of fine, top-quality copies on all types of finished paper.

The xerox process reproduces an exact duplicate from an original. It is the fastest duplicating method because the original material is placed directly on the duplicator, eliminating the need to make a special master. Any kind of paper can be used. The xerox process is the most expensive duplicating process; however, it is the best method of reproducing small quantities of good-quality copies of reports, letters, official documents, memos, or contracts.

1. Of the following, the MOST efficient method of reproducing 5,000 copies of a graph is 1.____
   A. stencil B. fluid C. offset D. Xerox

2. The offset process is the MOST adaptable office duplicating process because 2.____
   A. it is the quickest duplicating method
   B. it is the least expensive duplicating method
   C. it can produce a small number or large number of copies
   D. a softer master can be used over and over again

3. Which one of the following duplicating processes uses moistened paper? 3.____
   A. Stencil B. Fluid C. Offset D. Xerox

4. The fluid process would be the BEST process to use for reproducing 4.____
   A. five copies of a school transcript
   B. fifty copies of a memo
   C. five hundred copies of a form letter
   D. five thousand copies of a chart

5. Which one of the following duplicating processes does NOT require a special master? 5.____
   A. Fluid B. Xerox C. Offset D. Stencil

6. Xerox is NOT used for all duplicating jobs because 6.____
   A. it produces poor-quality copies
   B. the process is too expensive
   C. preparing the master is too time-consuming

Questions 7-10.

DIRECTIONS: Questions 7 through 10 are to be answered SOLELY on the basis of the information contained in the following passage.

City government is committed to providing a safe and healthy work environment for all city employees. An effective agency safety program reduces accidents by educating employees about the types of careless acts which can cause accidents. Even in an office, accidents can happen. If each employee is aware of possible safety hazards, the number of accidents on the job can be reduced.

Careless use of office equipment can cause accidents and injuries. For example, file cabinet drawers which are filled with papers can be so heavy that the entire cabinet could tip over from the weight of one open drawer.

The bottom drawers of desks and file cabinets should never be left open since employees could easily trip over open drawers and injure themselves.

When reaching for objects on a high shelf, an employee should use a strong, sturdy object such as a step stool to stand on. Makeshift platforms made out of books, papers, or boxes can easily collapse. Even chairs can slide out from under foot, causing serious injury.

Even at an employee's desk, safety hazards can occur. Frayed or cut wires should be repaired or replaced immediately. Typewriters which are not firmly anchored to the desk or table could fall, causing injury.

Smoking is one of the major causes of fires in the office. A lighted match or improperly extinguished cigarette thrown into a wastebasket filled with paper could cause a major fire with possible loss of life. Where smoking is permitted, ashtrays should be used. Smoking is particularly dangerous in offices where flammable chemicals are used.

7. The goal of an effective safety program is to 7.____
   A. reduce office accidents
   B. stop employees from smoking on the job
   C. encourage employees to continue their education
   D. eliminate high shelves in offices

8. Desks and file cabinets can become safety hazards when 8.____
   A. their drawers are left open
   B. they are used as wastebaskets
   C. they are makeshift
   D. they are not anchored securely to the floor

9. Smoking is especially hazardous when it occurs 9.____
   A. near exposed wires
   B. in a crowded office
   C. in an area where flammable chemicals are used
   D. where books and papers are stored

10. Accidents are likely to occur when 10.____
   A. employees' desks are cluttered with books and papers
   B. employees are not aware of safety hazards
   C. employees close desk drawers
   D. step stools are used to reach high objects

Questions 11-18.

DIRECTIONS: Questions 11 through 18 are to be answered SOLELY on the basis of the information contained in the following passage.

The telephone directory is made up of two books. The first book consists of the introductory section and the alphabetical listing of names section. The second book is the classified directly (also known as the yellow pages). Many people who are familiar with one book do not realize how useful the other can be. The efficient office worker should become familiar with both books in order to make the best use of this important source of information.

The introductory section gives general instructions for finding numbers in the alphabetical listing and classified directory. This section also explains how to use the telephone company's many services, including the operator and information services, gives examples of charges for local and long distance calls, and lists area codes for the entire country. In addition, this section provides a useful postal zip code map.

The alphabetical listing of names section lists the names, addresses, and telephone numbers of subscribers in an area. Guide names, or *telltales*, are on the top corner of each page. These guide names indicate the first and last name to be found on that page. *Telltales* help locate any particular name quickly. A cross-reference spelling is also given to help locate names which are spelled several different ways. City, state, and federal government agencies are listed under the major government heading. For example, an agency of the federal government would be listed under *United States Government*.

The classified directory, or yellow pages, is a separate book. In this section are advertising services, public transportation line maps, shopping guides, and listing of businesses arranged by the type of product or services they offer. This book is most useful when looking for the name or phone number of a business when all that is known is the type of product offered and the address, or when trying to locate a particular type of business in an area. Businesses listed in the classified directory can usually be found in the alphabetical listing of names section. When the name of the business is known, you will find the address or phone number more quickly in the alphabetical listing of names section.

11. The introductory section provides 11.____
    A. shopping guides
    B. government listings
    C. business listings
    D. information services

12. Advertising services would be found in the 12.____
    A. introductory section
    B. alphabetical listing of names section
    C. classified directory
    D. information services

13. According to the information in the above passage for locating government agencies, the Information Office of the Department of Consumer Affairs of New York city government would be alphabetically listed FIRST under 13.____
    A. *I* for Information Offices
    B. *D* for Department of Consumer Affairs
    C. *N* for New York City
    D. *G* for government

14. When the name of a business is known, the QUICKEST way to find the phone number is to look in the 14.____
    A. classified directory
    B. introductory section
    C. alphabetical listing of names section
    D. advertising service section

15. The QUICKEST way to find the phone number of a business when the type of service a business offers and its address is known is to look in the 15.____
    A. classified directory
    B. alphabetical listing of names section
    C. introductory section
    D. information service

16. What is a *telltale*? 16.____
A(n)
    A. alphabetical listing
    B. guide name
    C. map
    D. cross-reference listing

17. The BEST way to find a postal zip code is to look in the 17.____
    A. classified directory
    B. introductory section
    C. alphabetical listing of names section
    D. government heading

18. To help find names which have several different spellings, the telephone directory provides 18.____
    A. cross-reference spelling
    B. *telltales*
    C. spelling guides
    D. advertising services

Questions 19-24.

DIRECTIONS: Questions 19 through 24 are to be answered SOLELY on the basis of the information contained in the following instructions on sweeping.

SWEEPING

All sweeping must be done with damp sawdust, which is used to prevent the raising of dust when sweeping platforms and mezzanines. Soak sawdust thoroughly in a bucket of water for two to three hours before use. Drain before use so that no stains are left on concrete from excess water. In order to keep sawdust moist while being used, spread for an area of 120 feet in advance of actual sweeping. Never sweep sawdust over drains. To assure good footing, do not spread it on stairways or on damp or wet floor areas.

19. Dampened sawdust should be used when 19.____
    A. scrapping
    B. dusting
    C. sweeping
    D. mopping

20. Of the following procedures, which is the CORRECT order to be followed when sweeping with sawdust? 20.____
    A. Soak, drain, and spread
    B. Spread, drain, and soak
    C. Spread, soak, and drain
    D. Drain, spread, and soak

21. Of the following, it is MOST correct to soak the sawdust in a bucket of water for _____ hour(s). 21.____
    A. a half-hour to an
    B. one to two
    C. two to three
    D. three to four

22. The water should be drained from the bucket of sawdust so that excess water does NOT 22.____
    A. cause passengers to lose their footing
    B. stain the concrete
    C. flood the tracks
    D. slow down the sweeping

23. Sawdust is dampened in order to 23.____
    A. assure good footing on stairways
    B. prevent the raising of dust when sweeping
    C. prevent the staining of concrete
    D. cool off platforms

24. The dampened sawdust may be spread on 24.____
    A. wet floors B. drains C. stairways D. mezzanines

Questions 25-27.

DIRECTIONS: Questions 25 through 27 are to be answered SOLELY on the basis of the information contained in the following passage.

Whether a main lobby or upper corridor requires scrubbing or mopping and whether it should be done nightly or less frequently depends on the nature of the floor surface and the amount of traffic. In a building with heavy traffic, it may be desirable every night to scrub the main lobby and to mop the upper floor corridors. In such cases, it may also be found desirable to scrub the upper floors once a week. If traffic is light, it may be only necessary to mop the main lobby every other night and to mop the upper floor corridors once a week. If there is any traffic or usage at all, it will be necessary to at least sweep the corridors nightly.

25. According to the above passage, in a building with light traffic, the upper floor corridors should be 25.____
    A. swept every other night
    B. mopped every night
    C. swept nightly
    D. mopped every other night

26. According to the above passage, the number of times a floor is cleaned depends 26.____
    A. mainly on the type of floor surface
    B. mainly on the type of traffic
    C. only on the amount of traffic
    D. on both the floor surface and amount of traffic

27. According to the above passage, it may be DESIRABLE to have a heavily used main lobby swept 27.____
    A. daily and scrubbed weekly
    B. daily and mopped weekly
    C. and mopped weekly
    D. and scrubbed daily

Questions 28-30.

DIRECTIONS: Questions 28 through 30 are to be answered SOLELY on the basis of the information contained in the following passage.

<u>SENIOR CITIZEN AND HANDICAPPED PASSSENGER REDUCED FARE PROGRAM</u>

Upon display of his or her Medicare Card, Senior Citizen Reduced Fare Card, or Handicapped Photo I.D. Card to the Railroad Clerk on duty, and upon purchase of a token or evidence of having a token, a passenger will be issued a free return trip ticket. The passenger will then be directed to deposit full fare in a turnstile and enter the controlled area. Return trip tickets are valid 24 hours a day, 7 days a week, for the day of purchase and the following two (2) calendar days.

Each return trip ticket will be stamped with the station name and the date only at the time of issuing to a properly identified senior citizen or handicapped passenger. Overstamping of tickets is not allowed. Return trip tickets issued from 2300 hours will be stamped with the date of the following day.

On the return trip, the Railroad Clerk on duty will direct the passenger to enter the controlled area via the exit gate upon the passenger turning in the return trip ticket and displaying his/her Medicare Card, Senior Citizen Reduced Fare Card, or Handicapped Photo I.D. Card.

28. A Railroad Clerk issued a free return ticket to a senior citizen who displayed a birth certificate and a token. The Railroad Clerk's action was 28.____
   A. *proper*, because the Railroad Clerk had proof of the senior citizen's age
   B. *improper*, because the senior citizen did not display a Medicare Card, Senior Citizen Reduced Fair Card, or Handicapped Photo I.D. Card
   C. *proper*, because it is inconvenient for many senior citizens to obtain a Medicare Card, Senior Citizen Reduced Fare Card, or Handicapped Photo I.D. Card
   D. *improper*, because the senior citizen did not buy a token from the Railroad Clerk

29. The return trip ticket issued to a senior citizen is valid for ONLY 29.____
   A. 24 hours
   B. the day of purchase
   C. two days
   D. the day of purchase and the following two calendar days

30. A Railroad Clerk denied entry to the controlled area via the exit gate to an 18 year-old handicapped passenger who turned in a correctly stamped return trip ticket, but did not display any type of identification card. 30.____
   The Railroad Clerk's action was
   A. *proper*, because the passenger should have displayed his Handicapped Photo I.D. Card
   B. *improper*, because the passenger turned in a correctly stamped return trip ticket
   C. *proper*, because the passenger should have displayed either his Handicapped Photo I.D. Card or Social Security Card
   D. *improper*, because it should have been obvious to the Railroad Clerk that the passenger was handicapped

KEY (CORRECT ANSWERS)

1.	C	11.	D	21.	C
2.	C	12.	C	22.	B
3.	B	13.	C	23.	B
4.	B	14.	C	24.	D
5.	B	15.	A	25.	C
6.	A	16.	B	26.	D
7.	A	17.	B	27.	D
8.	A	18.	A	28.	B
9.	C	19.	C	29.	D
10.	B	20.	A	30.	A

TEST 2

DIRECTIONS: Each question or incomplete statement is followed by several suggested answers or completions. Select the one that BEST answers the question or completes the statement. *PRINT THE LETTER OF THE CORRECT ANSWER IN THE SPACE AT THE RIGHT.*

Questions 1-2.

DIRECTIONS: Questions 1 and 2 are to be answered SOLELY on the basis of the information contained in the following passage.

The Commissioner of Investigation shall have general responsibility for the investigation and elimination of corrupt or other criminal activity, conflicts of interest, unethical conduct, misconduct, and incompetence by city agencies, by city officers and employees, and by persons regulated by, doing business with, or receiving funds directly or indirectly from the city, with respect to their dealings with the city. All agency heads shall be responsible for establishing, subject to review for completeness and inter-agency consistency by the Commissioner of Investigation, written standards of conduct for the officials and employees of their respective agencies, and fair and efficient disciplinary systems to maintain those standards of conduct. All agencies shall have an Inspector General who shall report directly to the respective agency head and to the Commissioner of Investigation and be responsible for maintaining standards of conduct as may be established in such agency under this Order. Inspectors General shall be responsible for the investigation and elimination of corrupt or other criminal activity, conflicts of interest, unethical conduct, misconduct, and incompetence within their respective agencies. Except to the extent otherwise provided by law, the employment or continued employment of all existing and prospective Inspectors General and members of their staffs shall be subject to complete background investigations and approval by the Department of Investigation.

1. According to the above passage, establishing written standards of conduct for each agency is the responsibility of the 1.____
   A. agency head B. Commissioner of Investigation
   C. Department of Investigation D. Inspector General

2. According to the above passage, maintaining standards of conduct within each agency is the responsibility of the 2.____
   A. agency head B. Commissioner of Investigation
   C. Department of Investigation D. Inspector General

Questions 3-6.

DIRECTIONS: Questions 3 through 6 are to be answered SOLELY on the basis of the information contained in the following passage.

Assume that Warehouse X uses the following procedures for receiving stock. When a delivery is received, the stock handler who receives the delivery should immediately unpack and check the delivery. This check is to ensure that the quantity and kinds of stock items delivered match those on the purchase order which had been sent to the vendor. After the delivery is check, a receiving report is prepared by the same stock handler. This receiving report should include the name of the shipper, the purchase order number, the description of the item, and the actual count or weight of the item. The receiving report, along with the packing slip, should then be checked by the stores clerk against the purchase order to make sure that the quantity received is correct. This is necessary before credit can be obtained from the vendor for any items that are missing or damaged. After the checking is completed, the stock items can be moved to the stockroom.

3. According to the procedures described above, the stock person who receives the delivery should 3.____
   A. place the unopened delivery in a secure area for checking at a later date
   B. notify the stores clerk that the delivery has arrived and is ready for checking
   C. unpack the delivery and check the quantity and types of stock items against the purchase order
   D. closely examine the outside of the delivery containers for dents and damages

4. According to the procedures described above, credit can be obtained from the vendor 4.____
   A. *before* the stock handler checks the delivery of stock items
   B. *after* the stock handler checks the delivery of stock items
   C. *before* the stores clerk checks the receiving report against the purchase order
   D. *after* the stores clerk checks the receiving report against the purchase order

5. According to the procedures described above, all of the following information should be included when filling out a receiving report EXCEPT the 5.____
   A. purchase order number
   B. name of the shipper
   C. count or weight of the item
   D. unit cost per item

6. According to the procedures described above, after the stores clerk has checked the receiving report against the purchase order, the NEXT step is to 6.____
   A. move the stock items to the stockroom
   B. return the stock items received to the vendor
   C. give the stock items to the stock handler for final checking
   D. file the packing slip for inventory purposes

Questions 7-9.

DIRECTIONS: Questions 7 through 9 are to be answered SOLELY on the basis of the information contained in the following passage.

A filing system for requisition forms used in a warehouse will be of maximum benefit only if it provides ready access to information needed and is not too complex. How effective the system will be depends largely on how well the filing system is organized. A well-organized system usually results in a smooth-running operation.

When setting up a system for filing requisition forms, one effective method would be to first make an alphabetical listing of all the authorized requisitioning agencies. Then file folders should be prepared for each of these agencies and arranged alphabetically in file cabinets. Following this, each agency should be assigned a series of numbers corresponding to those on the blank requisition forms with which they will be supplied. When an agency then submits a requisition and it is filled, the form should be filed in numerical order in the designated agency folder. By using this system, any individual requisition form which is missing from its folder can be easily detected. Regardless of the filing system used, simplicity is essential if the filing system is to be successful.

7. According to the above passage, a filing system is MOST likely to be successful if it is 7.____
   A. alphabetical
   B. uncomplicated
   C. numerical
   D. reliable

8. According to the above passage, the reason numbers are assigned to each agency is to 8.____
   A. simplify stock issuing procedures
   B. keep a count of all incoming requisition forms
   C. be able to know when a form is missing from its folder
   D. eliminate the need for an alphabetical filing system

9. According to the above passage, which one of the following is an ACCURATE statement regarding the establishment of a well-organized filing system? 9.____
   A. Requisitioned stock items will be issued at a faster rate.
   B. Stock items will be stored in storage areas alphabetically arranged.
   C. Information concerning ordered stock items will be easily obtainable.
   D. Maximum productivity can be expected from each employee.

Questions 10-13.

DIRECTIONS: Questions 10 through 13 are to be answered SOLELY on the basis of the information contained in the following passage.

On Tuesday, October 21, Protection Agent Williams, on duty at the Jamaica Depot, observed a man jump over the fence and into the parking lot at 2:12 P.M. and run to a car that was parked with the engine running. The man, who limped slightly, opened the car door, jumped into the car, and sped out of the yard. The car was a 2018 gray Buick Electra, license plate 563-JYN, with parking decal No. 6043. The man was white, about 6 feet tall, about 175 pounds, in his mid-20's, with a scar on his left cheek. He wore a blue sportcoat, tan slacks, a white shift open at the neck with no tie, and brown loafers.

10. What was the color of the car? 10.____
   A. White
   B. Blue
   C. Two-tone brown and tan
   D. Gray

11. What were the distinguishing personal features of the man who jumped over the fence? 11.___
    A. A scar on the left cheek
    B. Pockmarks on his face
    C. A cast on his left wrist
    D. Bushy eyebrows

12. What was the number on the car's parking decal? 12.___
    A. 2018
    B. 673-JYN
    C. 6043
    D. 175

13. On what day of the week did the incident occur? 13.___
    A. Monday
    B. Tuesday
    C. Wednesday
    D. Sunday

14. *It is a violation of rules for a Protection Agent to carry a firearm while on Transit Authority property. The possession of such a weapon, whether carried on the person, in a personal vehicle, or stored in a locker, can result in charges being filed against the Agent.* 14.___
    According to the above information, the carrying of a firearm
    A. on Authority property by any employee is prohibited
    B. anywhere by an Agent is prohibited under all circumstances
    C. on Authority property by an Agent is prohibited under all circumstances
    D. anywhere by an Authority employee may be reason for charges being filed against that employee

15. *News reporters may enter Authority property if they have the written authorization of a Public Affairs Department official. The Agent on duty must get permission from the Property Protection Control Desk before admitting to the property a news person who has no such written authorization.* 15.___
    If a reporter tells a Protection Agent that she has received permission from the Authority President to enter the property, what is the FIRST thing the Agent should do?
    A. Call the Authority police.
    B. Admit the reporter immediately.
    C. Call the Authority President's office.
    D. Call the Property Protection Control Desk.

Questions 16-20.

DIRECTIONS: Questions 16 through 20 are to be answered SOLELY on the basis of the information contained in the following passage.

FIRES AND EXTINGUISHERS

There are four classes of fires.

Trash fires, paper fires, cloth fires, wood fires, etc. are classified as Class A fires. Water or a water-base solution should be used to extinguish Class A fires. They also can be extinguished by covering the combustibles with a multi-purpose dry chemical.

Burning liquids, gasoline, oil, paint, tar, etc. are considered Class B fires. Such fires can be extinguished by smothering or blanketing them. Extinguishers used for Class B fires are Halon, CO_2, or multi-purpose dry chemical. Water tends to spread such fires and should not be used.

Fires in electrical equipment and switchboards are classified as Class C fires. When live electrical equipment is involved, a non-conducting extinguishing agent like CO_2, a multi-purpose dry chemical, or Halon should always be used. Soda-acid or other water-type extinguishers should not be used.

Class D fires consist of burning metals in finely-divided forms like chips, turnings, and shavings. Specially-designed extinguishing agents that provide a smothering blanket or coating should be used to extinguish Class D fires. Multi-purpose dry-powder extinguishants are such agents.

16. The ONLY type of extinguishing agent that can be used on any type of fire is 16.____
    A. a multi-purpose, dry-chemical extinguishing agent
    B. soda-acid
    C. water
    D. carbon dioxide

17. A fire in litter swept from a subway car in a yard is MOST likely to be a Class _____ fire. 17.____
    A. A B. B C. C D. D

18. Fire coming from the underbody of a subway car is MOST likely to be a Class _____ fire. 18.____
    A. A B. B C. C D. D

19. Which of the following extinguishing agents should NOT be used in fighting a Class C fire involving live electrical equipment? 19.____
    A. Halon B. Carbon dioxide
    C. A multi-purpose dry chemical D. Soda-acid

20. Water is NOT recommended for use on Class B fires because water 20.____
    A. would cool the fire B. evaporates too quickly
    C. might spread the fire D. would smother the fire

Questions 21-24.

DIRECTIONS: Questions 21 through 24 are to be answered SOLELY on the basis of the information contained in the following passage.

Protection Agent Brown, working the midnight to 8:00 A.M. tour at the Flushing Bus Depot, discovered a fire at 2:17 A.M. in Bus No. 4651, which was parked in the southeast portion of the depot yard. He turned in an alarm to the Fire Department from Box 3297 on the nearby street at 2:18 A.M. At 2:20 A.M., he called the Property Protection Control Desk and reported the fire and his action to Line Supervisor Wilson. Line Supervisor Wilson instructed Agent Brown to lock his booth and go to the fire alarm box to direct the fire companies. The first arriving companies were Engine 307 and Ladder 154. Brown directed them to the burning bus. Two minutes later, at 2:23 A.M. Battalion Chief Welsh arrived from Battalion 14. The fire had made little headway. It was extinguished in about two minutes. Brown then wrote a fire report for submittal to Line Supervisor Wilson.

21. What was the FIRST thing Protection Agent Brown did after observing the fire? He 21.____
    A. called Battalion Chief Welsh
    B. called the Fire Dispatcher
    C. transmitted an alarm from a nearby alarm box
    D. called 911

22. In what part of the yard was the burning bus? 22.____
    A. Northeast section
    B. Southwest end
    C. Northwest part
    D. Southeast portion

23. What time did Agent Brown call Line Supervisor Wilson? 23.____
    A. 2:18 P.M.
    B. 2:20 A.M.
    C. 2:29 A.M.
    D. 2:36 A.M.

24. Which of the following CORRECTLY describes the sequence of Agent Brown's actions? He 24.____
    A. saw the fire, turned in an alarm, called the Property Protection Control Desk, directed the fire companies to the fire, and wrote a report
    B. called the Property Protection Control Desk, directed the fire apparatus, directed Chief Welsh, and wrote a report
    C. called Line Supervisor Wilson, turned in an alarm, waited by the burning bus, and directed the fire companies
    D. called Line Supervisor Wilson, directed the firefighters, waited for instructions from Line Supervisor Wilson, and wrote a report

Questions 25-26.

DIRECTIONS: Questions 25 and 26 are to be answered SOLELY on the basis of the information contained in the following passage.

Protection Agents may admit to Transit Authority headquarters only persons with Transit Authority passes, persons with job appointment letters, and persons who have permission to enter from Transit Authority officials.

During his tour in the Authority's headquarters lobby, Protection Agent Williams admitted to the building 326 persons with Authority passes and 41 persons with job appointment letters. He telephoned authorized officials for permission to admit 14 others, 13 of whom were granted permission and entered and one of whom was denied permission. He also turned away two persons who wanted to enter to sell to employees merchandise for their personal use, and one person who appeared inebriated.

25. How many persons did Agent Williams admit to the building? 25.____
A. 326 B. 367 C. 380 D. 382

26. To how many persons did Agent Williams refuse admittance? 26.____
A. 4 B. 13 C. 14 D. 41

Questions 27-30.

DIRECTIONS: Questions 27 through 30 are to be answered SOLELY on the basis of the information contained in the following instructions on Lost Property.

LOST PROPERTY

All inquiries for information regarding lost property will be referred to the Lost Property Office. Any Station Department employee finding a lost article, of any description, will immediately hand it over to the railroad clerk in the nearest 24-hour booth of the station where the article is found. The clerk must give the employee a receipt for the article. Should a passenger hand over a lost article to a cleaner, the cleaner will offer to escort the passenger to the nearest 24-hour booth in order that a receipt may be given by the railroad clerk there. If the passenger declines, the cleaner will accept the lost article without giving a receipt and proceed as desired above. Each employee who receive lost property will be held responsible for it unless he produces a receipt for it from another employee. Should any lost property disappear, the last employee who signed for it will be held accountable.

27. If a cleaner turns in a lost article to a railroad clerk in the nearest 24-hour booth, he should make sure that he 27.____
A. gets a receipt for the article
B. notifies his supervisor about the lost article
C. finds out the name of the owner of the article
D. writes a report on the incident

28. If a lost article disappears after a cleaner has properly turned it in to the railroad clerk in the nearest 24-hour booth, the one who will be held accountable is the 28.____
A. person who found the lost article
B. cleaner who turned in the article
C. supervisor in charge of the station
D. last employee to sign a receipt for the article

29. A passenger finds a lost article and gives it to a cleaner. The cleaner gives the passenger a receipt. 29.____
The cleaner's action was
A. *proper*, because the passenger was relieved of any responsibility for the lost article
B. *improper*, because the cleaner should have offered to escort the passenger to the nearest 24-hour booth
C. *proper*, because the cleaner is required to give the passenger a receipt
D. *improper*, because the cleaner should have sent the passenger to the Lost Property Office

30. A cleaner finds a five dollar bill on a crowded station platform. Three passengers who see him pick it up rush up and claim the money. The first passenger said he had just taken a roll of bills out of his pocket and must have dropped it. The second said he had just given two five dollar bills to his wife, and she had dropped one of them. The third said he had a hole in his pocket and the bill fell out of it. 30.____
The cleaner should
   A. give the five dollar bill t the second passenger because he had his wife as a witness
   B. give the five dollar bill to the third passenger because he had a hole in his pocket
   C. keep the five dollar bill
   D. bring the five dollar bill to the railroad clerk in the nearest 24-hour booth

KEY (CORRECT ANSWERS)

1.	A	11.	A	21.	C
2.	D	12.	C	22.	D
3.	C	13.	B	23.	B
4.	D	14.	C	24.	A
5.	D	15.	D	25.	C
6.	A	16.	A	26.	A
7.	B	17.	A	27.	A
8.	C	18.	C	28.	D
9.	C	19.	D	29.	B
10.	D	20.	C	30.	D

PREPARING WRITTEN MATERIAL

PARAGRAPH REARRANGEMENT COMMENTARY

The sentences that follow are in scrambled order. You are to rearrange them in proper order and indicate the letter choice containing the correct answer at the space at the right.

Each group of sentences in this section is actually a paragraph presented in scrambled order. Each sentence in the group has a place in that paragraph; no sentence is to be left out. You are to read each group of sentences and decide upon the best order in which to put the sentences so as to form a well-organized paragraph.

The questions in this section measure the ability to solve a problem when all the facts relevant to its solution are not given.

More specifically, certain positions of responsibility and authority require the employee to discover connection between events sometimes, apparently, unrelated. In order to do this, the employee will find it necessary to correctly infer that unspecified events have probably occurred or are likely to occur. This ability becomes especially important when action must be taken on incomplete information.

Accordingly, these questions require competitors to choose among several suggested alternatives, each of which presents a different sequential arrangement of the events. Competitors must choose the MOST logical of the suggested sequences.

In order to do so, they may be required to draw on general knowledge to infer missing concepts or events that are essential to sequencing the given events. Competitors should be careful to infer only what is essential to the sequence. The plausibility of the wrong alternatives will always require the inclusion of unlikely events or of additional chains of events which are NOT essential to sequencing the given events.

It's very important to remember that you are looking for the best of the four possible choices, and that the best choice of all may not even be one of the answers you're given to choose from.

There is no one right way to solve these problems. Many people have found it helpful to first write out the order of the sentences, as they would have arranged them, on their scrap paper before looking at the possible answers. If their optimum answer is there, this can save them some time. If it isn't, this method can still give insight into solving the problem. Others find it most helpful to just go through each of the possible choices, contrasting each as they go along. You should use whatever method feels comfortable and works for you.

While most of these types of questions are not that difficult, we've added a higher percentage of the difficult type, just to give you more practice. Usually there are only one or two questions on this section that contain such subtle distinctions that you're unable to answer confidently. And you then may find yourself stuck deciding between two possible choices, neither of which you're sure about.

PREPARING WRITTEN MATERIAL

EXAMINATION SECTION

TEST 1

DIRECTIONS: The following groups of sentences need to be arranged in an order that makes sense. Select the letter preceding the sequence that represents the BEST sentence order. *PRINT THE LETTER OF THE CORRECT ANSWER IN THE SPACE AT THE RIGHT.*

1. I. A large Naval station on Alameda Island, near Oakland, held many warships in port, and the War Department was worried that if the bridge were to be blown up by the enemy, passage to and from the bay would be hopelessly blocked. 1.____
   II. Though many skeptics were opposed to the idea of building such an enormous bridge, the most vocal opposition came from a surprising source: the United States War Department.
   III. The War Department's concerns led to a showdown at San Francisco City Hall between Strauss and the Secretary of War, who demanded to know what would happen if a military enemy blew up the bridge.
   IV. In 1933, by submitting a construction cost estimate of $17 million, an engineer named Joseph Strauss won the contract to build the Golden Gate Bridge of San Francisco, which would then become one of the world's largest bridges.
   V. Strauss quickly ended the debate by explaining that the Golden Gate Bridge was to be a suspension bridge, whose roadway would hang in the air from cables strung between two huge towers, and would immediately sink into three hundred feet of water if it were destroyed.
   The BEST order is:
   A. II, III, I, IV, V   B. I, II, III, V, IV   C. IV, II, I, III, V   D. IV, I, III, V, II

2. I. Plastic surgeons have already begun to use virtual reality to map out the complex nerve and tissue structures of a particular patient's face, in order to prepare for delicate surgery. 2.____
   II. A virtual reality program responds to these movements by adjusting the images that a person sees on a screen or through goggles, thereby creating an "interactive" world in which a person can see and touch three-dimensional graphic objects.
   III. No more than a computer program that is designed to build and display graphic images, the virtual reality program takes graphic programs a step further by sensing a person's head and body movements.
   IV. The computer technology known as virtual reality, now in its very first stages of development, is already revolutionizing some aspects of contemporary life.
   V. Virtual reality computers are also being used by the space program, most recently to simulate conditions for the astronauts who were launched on a repair mission to the Hubble telescope.

The BEST order is:
A. IV, II, I, V, III B. III, I, V, II, IV C. IV, III, II, I, V D. III, I, II, IV, V

3. I. Before you plant anything, the soil in your plant bed should be carefully raked level, a small section at a time, and any clods or rocks that can't be broken up should be removed. 3.____
II. Your plant should be placed in a hole that will position it at the same level it was at the nursery, and a small indentation should be pressed into the soil around the plant in order to hold water near its roots.
III. Before placing the plant in the soil, lightly separate any roots that may have been matted together in the container, cutting away any thick masses that can't be separated, so that the remaining roots will be able to grow outward.
IV. After the bed is ready, remove your plant from its container by turning it upside down and tapping or pushing on the bottom —never remove it by pulling on the plant.
V. When you bring home a small plant in an individual container from the nursery, there are several things to remember while preparing to plant it in your own garden.

The BEST order is:
A. V, IV, III, II, I B. V, II, IV, III, II C. I, IV, II, III, V D. I, IV, V, II, III

4. I. The motte and its tower were usually built first, so that sentries could use it as a lookout to warn the castle workers of any danger that might approach the castle. 4.____
II. Though the moat and palisade offered the bailey a good deal of protection, it was linked to the motte by a set of stairs that led to a retractable drawbridge at the motte's gate, to enable people to evacuate onto the motte in case of an attack.
III. The motte of these early castles was a fortified hill, sometimes as high as one hundred feet, on which stood a palisade and tower.
IV. The bailey was a clear, level spot below the motte, also enclosed by a palisade, which in turn was surrounded by a large trench or moat.
V. The earliest castles built in Europe were not the magnificent stone giants that still tower over much of the European landscape, but simpler wooden constructions called motte-and-bailey castles.

The BEST order is:
A. V, III, I, IV, II B. V, IV, I, II, III C. I, IV, III, II, V D. I, III, II, IV, V

5. I. If an infant is left alone or abandoned for a short while, its immediate response is to cry loudly, accompanying its screams with aggressive flailing of its legs and limbs. 5.____
II. If a child has been abandoned for a longer period of time, it becomes completely still and quiet, as if realizing that now its only chance for survival is to shut its mouth and remain motionless.
III. Along with their intense fear of the dark, the crying behavior of human infants offers insights into how prehistoric newborn children might have evolved instincts that would prevent them from becoming victims of predators.

IV. This behavior often surprises people who enter a hospital's maternity ward for the first time and encounter total silence from a roomful of infants.
V. This violent screaming response is quite different from an infant's cries of discomfort or hunger, and seems to serve as either the child's first line of defense against an unwanted intruder, or a desperate attempt to communicate its position to the mother.

The BEST order is:
A. III, II, IV, I, V B. III, I, V, II, IV C. I, V, IV, II, III D. II, IV, I, V, III

6. I. When two cats meet who are strangers, their first actions and gestures determine who the "dominant" cat will be, at least for the time being. 6.____
II. Unlike dogs, cats are typically a solitary animal species who avoid social interaction, but they do display specific social responses to each other upon meeting.
III. This is unlikely, however; before such a point of open hostility is reached, one of the cats will usually take the "submissive" position of crouching down while looking away from the other dat.
IV. If a cat desires dominance or sees the other cat as a threat to its territory, it will stare directly at the intruder with a lowered tail.
V. If the other cat responds with a similar gesture, or with the strong defensive posture of an arched back, laid-back ears and raised tail, a fight or chase is likely if neither cat gives in.

The BEST order is:
A. IV, II, I, V, III B. I, II, IV, V, III C. I, IV, V, III, II D. II, I, IV, V, III

7. I. A star or planet's gravitational force can best be explained in this way: anything passing through this "dent" in space will veer toward the star or planet as if it were rolling into a hole. 7.____
II. Objects that are massive or heavy, such as stars or planets, "sink" into this surface, creating a sort of dent or concavity in the surrounding space.
III. Black holes, the most massive objects known to exist in space, create dents so large and deep that the space surrounding them actually folds in on itself, preventing anything that falls in —even light —from ever escaping again.
IV. The sort of dent a star or planet makes depends on how massive it is; planets generally have weak gravitational pulls, but stars, which are larger and heavier, make a bigger "dent" that will attract more matter.
V. In outer space, the force of gravity works as if the surrounding space is a soft, flat surface.

The BEST order is:
A. III, V, II, I, IV B. III, IV, I, V, II C. V, II, I, IV, III D. I, V, II, IV, III

8. I. Eventually, the society of Kyoto gave the world one of its first and greatest novels when Japan's most promising writer, Lady Murasaki Shikibu, wrote her chronicle of Kyoto's society, *The Tale of Genji*, which preceded the first European novels by more than 500 years. 8.____
II. The society of Kyoto was dedicated to the pleasures of art; the courtiers experimented with new and colorful methods of sculpture, painting, writing, decorative gardening, and even making clothes.

III. Japanese culture began under the powerful authority of Chinese Buddhism, which influenced every aspect of Japanese life from religion to politics and art.
IV. This new, vibrant culture was so sophisticated that all the people in Kyoto's imperial court considered themselves poets, and the line between life and art hardly existed —lovers corresponded entirely through written verses, and even government officials communicated by writing poems to each other.
V. In the eighth century, when the emperor established the town of Kyoto as the capital of the Japanese empire, Japanese society began to develop its own distinctive style.

The BEST order is:
A. V, II, IV, I, III B. II, I, V, IV, III C. V, III, IV, I, II D. III, V, II, IV, I

9. I. Instead of wheels, the HSST uses two sets of magnets, one which sits on the track, and another that is carried by the train; these magnets generate an identical magnetic field which forces the two sets apart. 9.____
II. In the last few decades, railway travel has become less popular throughout the world, because it is much slower than travel by airplane, and not much less expensive.
III. The HSST's designers say that the train can take passengers from one town to another as quickly as a jet plane —while consuming less than half the energy.
IV. This repellent effect is strong enough to lift the entire train above the trackway, and the train, literally traveling on air, rockets along at speeds of up to 300 miles per hour.
V. The revolutionary technology of magnetic levitation, currently being tested by Japan's experimental HSST (High Speed Surface Transport), may yet bring passenger trains back from the dead.

The BEST order is:
A. II, V, I, IV, III B. II, I, IV, III, V C. V, II, III, I, IV D. V, I, III, IV, II

10. I. When European countries first began to colonize the African continent, their impression of the African people was of a vast group of loosely organized tribal societies, without any great centralized source of power or wealth. 10.____
II. The legend of Timbuktu persisted until the nineteenth century, when a French adventurer visited Timbuktu and found that raids by neighboring tribesmen had made the city a shadow of its former self.
III. In the fifteenth century, when the stories of travelers who had traveled Africa's Sudan region began circulating around Europe, this impression began to change.
IV. In 1470, an Italian merchant named Benedetto Dei traveled to Timbuktu and confirmed these rumors, describing a thriving metropolis where rich and poor people worshipped together in the city's many ornate mosques —there was even a university in Timbuktu, much like its European counterparts, where African scholars pursued their studies in the arts and sciences.

V. The travelers' legends told of an enormous city in the western Sudan, Timbuktu, where the streets were crowded with goods brought by faraway caravans, and where there was a stone palace as large as any in Europe.

The BEST order is:

A. III, V, I, IV, II B. I, II, IV, III, V C. I, III, V, IV, II D. II, I, III, IV, V

11. I. Also, our reference points in sighting the moon make us believe that its size is changing; when the moon is rising through the trees, it seems huge, because our brains unconsciously compare the size of the moon with the size of the trees in the foreground. 11.____

II. To most people, the sky itself appears more distant at the horizon than directly overhead, and if the moon's size—which remains constant—is projected from the horizon, the apparent distance of the horizon makes the moon look bigger.

III. Up higher in the sky, the moon is set against tiny stars in the background, which will make the moon seem smaller.

IV. People often wonder why the moon becomes bigger when it approaches the horizon, but most scientists agree that this is a complicated optical illusion, produced by at least three factors.

V. The moon illusion may also be partially explained by a phenomenon that has nothing to do with errors in our perception—light that enters the earth's atmosphere is sometimes refracted, and so the atmosphere may act as a kind of magnifying glass for the moon's image.

The BEST order is:

A. IV, III, V, II, I B. IV, II, I, III, V C. V, II, I, III, IV D. II, I, III, IV, V

12. I. When the Native Americans were introduced to the horses used by white explorers, they were amazed at their new alternative—here was an animal that was strong and swift, would patiently carry a person or other loads on its back, and they later discovered, was right at home on the plains. 12.____

II. Before the arrival of European explorers to North America, the natives of the American plains used large dogs to carry their travois-long lodgepoles loaded with clothing, gear, and food.

III. These horses, it is now known, were not really strangers to North America; the very first horses originated here, on this continent, tens of thousands of years ago, and migrated into Asia across the Bering Land Bridge, a strip of land that used to link our continent with the Eastern world.

IV. At first, the natives knew so little about horses that at least one tribe tried to feed their new animals pieces of dried meat and animal fat, and were surprised when the horses turned their heads away and began to eat the grass of the prairie.

V. The American horse eventually became extinct, but its Asian cousins were reintroduced to the New World when the European explorers brought them to live among the Native Americans.

The BEST order is:

A. II, I, IV, III, V B. II, IV, I, III, V C. I, II, IV, III, V D. I, III, V, II, IV

13. I. The dress worn by the dancer is believed to have been adorned in the past by shells which would strike each other as the dancer performed, creating a lovely sound. 13.____
    II. Today's jingle-dress is decorated with the tin lids of snuff cans, which are rolled into cones and sewn onto the dress,
    III. During the jingle-dress dance, the dancer must blend complicated footwork with a series of gentle hos that cause the cones to jingle in rhythm to a drumbeat.
    IV. When contemporary Native American tribes meet for a pow-wow, one of the most popular ceremonies to take place is the women's jingle-dress dance.
    V. Besides being more readily available than shells, the lids are thought by many dancers to create a softer, more subtle sound.
    The BEST order is:
    A. II, IV, V, I, III B. IV, II, I, III, V C. II, I, III, V, IV D. IV, I, II, V, III

14. I. If a homeowner lives where seasonal climates are extreme, deciduous shade trees—which will drop their leaves in the winter and allow sunlight to pass through the windows—should be planted near the southern exposure in order to keep the house cool during the summer. 14.____
    II. This trajectory is shorter and lower in the sky than at any other time of year during the winter, when a house most requires heating; the northern-facing parts of a house do not receive any direct sunlight at all.
    III. In designing an energy-efficient house, especially in colder climates, it is important to remember that most of the house's windows should face south.
    IV. Though the sun always rises in the east and sets in the west, the sun of the northern hemisphere is permanently situated in the southern portion of the sky.
    V. The explanation for why so many architects and builders want this "southern exposure" is related to the path of the sun in the sky.
    The BEST order is:
    A. III, I, V, IV, II B. III, V, IV, II, I C. I, III, IV, II, V D. I, II, V, IV, III

15. I. His journeying lasted twenty-four years and took him over an estimated 75,000 miles, a distance that would not be surpassed by anyone other than Magellan—who sailed around the world—for another six hundred years. 15.____
    II. Perhaps the most far-flung of these lesser-known travelers was Ibn Batuta, an African Moslem who left his birthplace of Tangier in the summer of 1325.
    III. Ibn Batuta traveled all over Africa and Asia, from Niger to Peking, and to the islands of Maldive and Indonesia.
    IV. However, a few explorers of the Eastern world logged enough miles and adventures to make Marco Polo's voyage look like an evening stroll.
    V. In America, the most well-known of the Old World's explorers are usually Europeans such as Marco Polo, the Italian who brought many elements of Chinese culture to the Western world.
    The BEST order is:
    A. V, IV, II, III, I B. V, IV, III, II, I C. III, II, I, IV, V D. II, III, I, IV, V

16. I. In the rainforests of South America, a rare species of frog practices a reproductive method that is entirely different from this standard process. 16.____
II. She will eventually carry each of the tadpoles up into the canopy and drop each into its own little pool, where it will be easy to locate and safe from most predators.
III. After fertilization, the female of the species, who lives almost entirely on the forest floor, lays between 2 and 16 eggs among the leaf litter at the base of a tree, and stands watch over these eggs until they hatch.
IV. Most frogs are pond-dwellers who are able to deposit hundreds of eggs in the water and then leave them alone, knowing that enough eggs have been laid to insure the survival of some of their offspring.
V. Once the tadpoles emerge, the female backs in among them, and a tadpole will wriggle onto her back to be carried high into the forest canopy, where the female will deposit it in a little pool of water cupped in the leaf of a plant.
The BEST order is:
A. I, IV, III, II, V B. I, III, V, II, IV C. IV, III, II, V, I D. IV, I, III, V, II

17. I. Eratosthenes had heard from travelers that at exactly noon on June 21, in the ancient city of Aswan, Egypt, the sun cast no shadow in a well, which meant that the sun must be directly overhead. 17.____
II. He knew the sun always cast a shadow in Alexandria, and so he figured that if he could measure the length of an Alexandria shadow at the time when there was no shadow in Aswan, he could calculate the angle of the sun, and therefore the circumference of the earth.
III. The evidence for a round earth was not new in 1492; in fact, Eratosthenes, an Alexandrian geographer who lived nearly sixteen centuries before Columbus's voyage (275-195 B.C.), actually developed a method for calculating the circumference of the earth that is still in use today.
IV. Eratosthenes's method was correct, but his result—28,700 miles—was about 15 percent too high, probably because of the inaccurate ancient methods of keeping time, and because Aswan was not due south of Alexandria, as Eratosthenes had believed.
V. When Christopher Columbus sailed across the Atlantic Ocean for the first time in 1492, there were still some people in the world who ignored scientific evidence and believed that the earth was flat, rather than round.
The BEST order is:
A. I, II, V, III, IV B. V, III, IV, I, II C. V, III, I, II, IV D. III, V, I, II, IV

18. I. The first name for the child is considered a trial naming, often impersonal and neutral, such as the Ngoni name *Chabwera*, meaning "it has arrived." 18.____
II. This sort of name is not due to any parental indifference to the child, but is a kind of silent recognition of Africa's sometimes high infant death rate; most parents ease the pain of losing a child with the belief that it is not really a person until it has been given a final name.
III. In many tribal African societies, families often give two different names to their children, at different periods in time.
IV. After the trial naming period has subsided and it is clear that the child will survive, the parents choose a final name for the child, an act that symbolically completes the act of birth.

V. In fact, some African first-given names are explicitly uncomplimentary, translating as "I am dead" or "I am ugly," in order to avoid the jealousy of ancestral spirits who might wish to take a child that is especially healthy or attractive.

The BEST order is:

A. III, I, II, V, IV B. III, IV, II, I, V C. IV, III, I, II, V D. IV, V, III, I, II

19. I. Though uncertain of the definite reasons for this behavior, scientists believe the birds digest the clay in order to counteract toxins contained in the seeds of certain fruits that are eaten by macaws. 19.____

II. For example, all macaws flock to riverbanks at certain times of the year to eat the clay that is found in river mud.

III. The macaws of South America are not only among the largest and most beautifully colored of the world's flying birds, but they are also one of the smartest.

IV. It is believed that macaws are forced to resort to these toxic fruits during the dry season, when foods are more scarce.

V. The macaw's intelligence has led to intense study by scientists, who have discovered some macaw behaviors that have not yet been explained.

The BEST order is:

A. III, IV, I, II, V B. III, V, II, I, IV C. V, II, I, IV, III D. IV, I, II, III, V

20. I. Although Maggie Kuhn has since passed away, the Gray Panthers are still waging a campaign to reinstate the historical view of the elderly as people whose experience allows them to make their greatest contribution in their later years. 20.____

II. In 1972, an elderly woman named Maggie Kuhn responded to this sort of treatment by forming a group called the Gray Panthers, an organization of both old and young adults with the common goal of creating change.

III. This attitude is reflected strongly in the way elderly people are treated by our society; many are forced into early retirement, or are placed in rest homes in which they are isolated from their communities.

IV. Unlike most other cultures around the world, Americans tend to look upon old age with a sense of dread and sadness.

V. Kuhn believed that when the elderly are forced to withdraw into lives that lack purpose, society loses one of its greatest resources: people who have a lifetime of experience and wisdom to offer their communities.

The BEST order is:

A. IV, III, II, V, I B. IV, II, I, III, V C. II, IV, III, V, I D. II, I, IV, III, V

21. I. The current theory among most anthropologists is that humans evolved from apes who lived in trees near the grasslands of Africa. 21.____

II. Still, some anthropologists insist that such an invention was necessary for the survival of early humans, and point to the Kung Bushmen of central Africa as a society in which the sling is still used in this way.

III. Two of these inventions—fire, and weapons such as spears and clubs—were obvious defenses against predators, and there is archaeological evidence to support the theory of their use.

IV. Once people had evolved enough to leave the safety of trees and walk upright, they needed the protection of several inventions in order to survive.
V. But another invention, a feather or fiber sling that allowed mothers to carry children while leaving their hands free to gather roots or berries, would certainly have decomposed and left behind no trace of itself.

The BEST order is:

A. I, II, III, V, IV B. IV, I, II, III, V C. I, IV, III, V, II D. IV, III, V, II, I

22. I. The person holding the bird should keep it in hot water up to its neck, and the person cleaning should work a mild solution of dishwashing liquid into the bird's plumage, paying close attention to the head and neck. 22.____
II. When rinsing the bird, after all the oil has been removed, the running water should be directed against the lay of its feathers, until water begins to bead off the surface of the feathers—a sign that all the detergent has been rinsed out.
III. If you have rescued a sea bird from an oil spill and want to restore it to clean and normal living, you need a large sink, a constant supply of running hot water (a little over 100ºF), and regular dishwashing liquid.
IV. This cleaning with detergent solution should be repeated as many times as it takes to remove all traces of oil from the bird's feathers, sometime over a period of several days.
V. But before you begin to clean the bird, you must find a partner because cleaning an oiled bird is a two-person job.

The BEST order is:

A. III, I, II, IV, V B. III, V, I, IV, II C. III, I, IV, V, II D. III, IV, V, I, II

23. I. The most difficult time of year for the Tsaatang is the spring calving, when the reindeer leave their wintering ground and rush to their accustomed calving place, without stopping by night or by day. 23.____
II. Reindeer travel in herds, and though some animals are tamed by the Tsaatang for riding or milking, the herds are allowed to roam free.
III. This journey is hard for the Tsaatang, who carry all their possessions with them, but once it's over it proves worthwhile; the Tsaatang can immediately begin to gather milk from reindeer cows who have given birth.
IV. The Tsaatang, a small tribe who live in the far northwest corner of Mongolia, practice a lifestyle that is completely dependent on the reindeer, their main resource for food, clothing, and transport.
V. The people must follow their yearly migrations, living in portable shelters that resemble Native American tepees.

The BEST order is:

A. I, III, II, V, IV B. I, IV, II, V, III C. IV, I, III, V, II D. IV II, V, I, III

24. I. The Romans later improved this system by installing these heated pipe networks throughout walls and ceilings, supplying heat to even the uppermost floors of a building—a system that, to this day, hasn't been much improved. 24.____
II. Air-conditioning, the method by which humans control indoor temperatures, was practiced much earlier than most people think.

III. The earliest heating devices other than open fires were used in 350 B.C. by the ancient Greeks, who directed air that had been heated by underground fires into baked clay pipes that ran under the floor.
IV. Ironically, the first successful cooling system, patented in England in 1831, used fire as its main energy source—fires were lit in the attic of a building, creating an updraft of air that drew cool air into the building through ducts that had underground openings near the river Thames.
V. Cooling buildings was more of a challenge, and wasn't attempted until 1500: a water-based system, designed by Leonardo da Vinci, does not appear to have been successful, since it was never used again.

The BEST order is:
A. III, V, IV, I, II B. III, I, II, V, IV C. II, III, I, V, IV D. IV, II, III, I, V

25. I. Cold, dry air from Canada passes over the Rocky Mountains and sweeps down onto the plains, where it collides with warm, moist air from the waters of the Gulf of Mexico, and when the two air masses meet, the resulting disturbance sometimes forms a violent funnel cloud that strikes the earth and destroys virtually everything in its path. 25.____
II. Hurricanes, storms which are generally not this violent and last much longer, are usually given names by meteorologists, but this tradition cannot be applied to tornados, which have a life span measured in minutes and disappear in the same way as they are born—unnamed.
III. A tornado funnel forms rotating columns of air whose speed reaches three hundred miles an hour—a speed that can only be estimated, because no wind-measuring devices in the direct path of a storm have ever survived.
IV. The natural phenomena known as tornados occur primarily over the Midwestern grasslands of the United States.
V. It is here, meteorologists tell us, that conditions for the formation of tornados are sometimes perfect during the spring months.

The BEST order is:
A. II IV, V, I, III B. II, III, I, V, IV C. IV, V, I, III, II D. IV, III, I, V, II

KEY (CORRECT ANSWERS)

1. C
2. C
3. B
4. A
5. B

6. D
7. C
8. D
9. A
10. C

11. B
12. A
13. D
14. B
15. A

16. D
17. C
18. A
19. B
20. A

21. C
22. B
23. D
24. C
25. C

EXAMINATION SECTION

TEST 1

DIRECTIONS: The following groups of sentences need to be arranged in an order that makes sense. Select the letter preceding the sequence that represents the BEST sentence order. *PRINT THE LETTER OF THE CORRECT ANSWER IN THE SPACE AT THE RIGHT.*

1. I. The keyboard was purposely designed to be a little awkward to slow typists down. 1.____
   II. The arrangement of letters on the keyboard of a typewriter was not designed for the convenience of the typist.
   III. Fortunately, no one is suggesting that a new keyboard be designed right away.
   IV. If one were, we would have to learn to type all over again.
   V. The reason was that the early machines were slower than the typists and would jam easily.

   The CORRECT answer is:

   A. I, III, IV, II, V
   B. II, V, I, IV, III
   C. V, I, II, III, IV
   D. II, I, V, III, IV

2. I. The majority of the new service jobs are part-time or low-paying. 2.____
   II. According to the U.S. Bureau of Labor Statistics, jobs in the service sector constitute 72% of all jobs in this country.
   III. If more and more workers receive less and less money, who will buy the goods and services needed to keep the economy going?
   IV. The service sector is by far the fastest growing part of the United States economy.
   V. Some economists look upon this trend with great concern.

   The CORRECT answer is:

   A. II, IV, I, V, III
   B. II, III, IV, I, V
   C. V, IV, II, III, I
   D. III, I, II, IV, V

3. I. They can also affect one's endurance. 3.____
   II. This can stabilize blood sugar levels, and ensure that the brain is receiving a steady, constant, supply of glucose, so that one is *hitting on all cylinders* while taking the test.
   III. By food, we mean real food, not junk food or unhealthy snacks.
   IV. For this reason, it is important not to skip a meal, and to bring food with you to the exam.
   V. One's blood sugar levels can affect how clearly one is able to think and concentrate during an exam.

   The CORRECT answer is:

   A. V, IV, II, III, I
   B. V, II, I, IV, III
   C. V, I, IV, III, II
   D. V, IV, I, III, II

4. I. Those who are the embodiment of desire are absorbed in material quests, and those who are the embodiment of feeling are warriors who value power more than possession. 4.____
II. These qualities are in everyone, but in different degrees.
III. But those who value understanding yearn not for goods or victory, but for knowledge.
IV. According to Plato, human behavior flows from three main sources: desire, emotion, and knowledge.
V. In the perfect state, the industrial forces would produce but not rule, the military would protect but not rule, and the forces of knowledge, the philosopher kings, would reign.
The CORRECT answer is:
A. IV, V, I, II, III
B. V, I, II, III, IV
C. IV, III, II, I, V
D. IV, II, I, III, V

5. I. Of the more than 26,000 tons of garbage produced daily in New York City, 12,000 tons arrive daily at Fresh Kills. 5.____
II. In a month, enough garbage accumulates there to fill the Empire State Building.
III. In 1937, the Supreme Court halted the practice of dumping the trash of New York City into the sea.
IV. Although the garbage is compacted, in a few years the mounds of garbage at Fresh Kills will be the highest points south of Maine's Mount Desert Island on the Eastern Seaboard.
V. Instead, tugboats now pull barges of much of the trash to Staten Island and the largest landfill in the world, Fresh Kills.
The CORRECT answer is:
A. III, V, IV, I, II
B. III, V, II, IV, I
C. III, V, I, II, IV
D. III, II, V, IV, I

6. I. Communists rank equality very high, but freedom very low. 6.____
II. Unlike communists, conservatives place a high value on freedom and a very low value on equality.
III. A recent study demonstrated that one way to classify people's political beliefs is to look at the importance placed on two words: freedom and equality.
IV. Thus, by demonstrating how members of these groups feel about the two words, the study has proved to be useful for political analysts in several European countries.
V. According to the study, socialists and liberals rank both freedom and equality very high, while fascists rate both very low.
The CORRECT answer is:
A. III, V, I, II, IV
B. V, IV, III, I, II
C. III, V, IV, II, I
D. III, I, II, IV, V

7. I. "Can there be anything more amazing than this?" 7.____
II. If the riddle is successfully answered, his dead brothers will be brought back to life.
III. "Even though man sees those around him dying every day," says Dharmaraj, "he still believes and acts as if he were immortal."
IV. "What is the cause of ceaseless wonder?" asks the Lord of the Lake.
V. In the ancient epic, The Mahabharata, a riddle is asked of one of the Pandava brothers.
The CORRECT answer is:
A. V, II, I, IV, III
B. V, IV, III, I, II
C. V, II, IV, III, I
D. V, II, IV, I, III

8. I. On the contrary, the two main theories—the cooperative (neoclassical) theory and the radical (labor theory)—clearly rest on very different assumptions, which have very different ethical overtones. 8.____
II. The distribution of income is the primary factor in determining the relative levels of material well-being that different groups or individuals attain.
III. Of all issues in economics, the distribution of income is one of the most controversial.
IV. The neoclassical theory tends to support the existing income distribution (or minor changes), while the labor theory ends to support substantial changes in the way income is distributed.
V. The intensity of the controversy reflects the fact that different economic theories are not purely neutral, *detached* theories with no ethical or moral implications.
The CORRECT answer is:
A. II, I, V, IV, III
B. III, II, V, I, IV
C. III, V, II, I, IV
D. III, V, IV, I, II

9. I. The pool acts as a broker and ensures that the cheapest power gets used first. 9.____
II. Every six seconds, the pool's computer monitors all of the generating stations in the state and decides which to ask for more power and which to cut back.
III. The buying and selling of electrical power is handled by the New York Power Pool in Guilderland, New York.
IV. This is to the advantage of both the buying and selling utilities.
V. The pool began operation in 1970, and consists of the state's eight electric utilities.
The CORRECT answer is:
A. V, I, II, III, IV
B. IV, II, I, III, V
C. III, V, I, IV, II
D. V, III, IV, II, I

10. I. Modern English is much simpler grammatically than Old English. 10.____
II. Finnish grammar is very complicated; there are some fifteen cases, for example.
III. Chinese, a very old language, may seem to be the exception, but it is the great number of characters/words that must be mastered that makes it so difficult to learn, not its grammar.
IV. The newest literary language—that is, written as well as spoken—is Finish, whose literary roots go back only to about the middle of the nineteenth century.
V. Contrary to popular belief, the longer a language is been in use the simpler its grammar—not the reverse.

The CORRECT answer is:
A. IV, I, II, III, V
B. V, I, IV, II, III
C. I, II, IV, III, V
D. IV, II, III, I, V

KEY (CORRECT ANSWERS)

1.	D	6.	A
2.	A	7.	C
3.	C	8.	B
4.	D	9.	C
5.	C	10.	B

TEST 2

DIRECTIONS: This type of question tests your ability to recognize accurate paraphrasing, well-constructed paragraphs, and appropriate style and tone. It is important that the answer you select contains only the facts or concepts given in the original sentences. It is also important that you be aware of incomplete sentences, inappropriate transitions, unsupported opinions, incorrect usage, and illogical sentence order. Paragraphs that do not include all the necessary facts and concepts, that distort them, or that add new ones are not considered correct.

The format for this section may vary. Sometimes, long paragraphs are given, and emphasis is placed on style and organization. Our first five questions are of this type. Other times, the paragraphs are shorter, and there is less emphasis on style and more emphasis on accurate representation of information. Our second group of five questions are of this nature.

For each of Questions 1 through 10, select the paragraph that BEST expresses the ideas contained in the sentences above it. *PRINT THE LETTER OF THE CORRECT ANSWER IN THE SPACE AT THE RIGHT.*

1. I. Listening skills are very important for managers. 1.____
II. Listening skills are not usually emphasized.
III. Whenever managers are depicted in books, manuals or the media, they are always talking, never listening.
IV. We'd like you to read the enclosed handout on listening skills and to try to consciously apply them this week.
V. We guarantee they will improve the quality of your interactions.

A. Unfortunately, listening skills are not usually emphasized for managers. Managers are always depicted as talking, never listening. We'd like you to read the enclosed handout on listening skills. Please try to apply these principles this week. If you do, we guarantee they will improve the quality of your interactions.
B. The enclosed handout on listening skills will be important improving the quality of your interactions. We guarantee it. All you have to do is take sometime this week to read and to consciously try to apply the principles. Listening skills are very important for manages, but they are not usually emphasized. Whenever managers are depicted in books, manuals or the media, they are always talking, never listening.
C. Listening well is one of the most important skills a manager can have, yet it's not usually given much attention. Think about any representation of managers in books, manuals, or in the media that you may have seen. They're always talking, never listening. We'd like you to read the enclosed handout on listening skills and consciously try to apply them the rest of the week. We guarantee you will see a difference in the quality of your interactions.

D. Effective listening, one very important tool in the effective manager's arsenal, is usually not emphasized enough. The usual depiction of managers in books, manuals or the media is one in which they are always talking, never listening. We'd like you to read the enclosed handout and consciously try to apply the information contained therein throughout the rest of the week. We feel sure that you will see a marked difference in the quality of your interactions.

2. I. Chekhov wrote three dramatic masterpieces which share certain themes and formats: Uncle Vanya, The Cherry Orchard, and The Three Sisters. 2.____
II. They are primarily concerned with the passage of time and how this erodes human aspirations.
III. The plays are haunted by the ghosts of the wasted life.
IV. The characters are concerned with life's lesser problems; however, such as the inability to make decisions, loyalty to the wrong cause, and the inability to be clear.
V. This results in sweet, almost aching, type of a sadness referred to as Chekhovian.

A. Chekhov wrote three dramatic masterpieces: Uncle Vanya, The Cherry Orchard, and The Three Sisters. These masterpieces share certain themes and formats: the passage of time, how time erodes human aspirations, and the ghosts of wasted life. Each masterpiece is characterized by a sweet, almost aching, type of sadness that has become known as Chekhovian. The sweetness of this sadness hinges on the fact that it is not the great tragedies of life which are destroying these characters, but their minor flaws: indecisiveness, misplaced loyalty, unclarity.
B. The Cherry Orchard, Uncle Vanya, and The Three Sisters are three dramatic masterpieces written by Chekhov that use similar formats to explore a common theme. Each is primarily concerned with the way that passing time wears down human aspirations, and each is haunted by the ghosts of the wasted life. The characters are shown struggling futilely with the lesser problems of life: indecisiveness, loyalty to the wrong cause, and the inability to be clear. These struggles create a mood of sweet, almost aching, sadness that has become known as Chekhovian.
C. Chekhov's dramatic masterpieces are, along with The Cherry Orchard, Uncle Vanya, and The Three Sisters. These plays share certain thematic and formal similarities. They are concerned most of all with the passage of time and the way in which time erodes human aspirations. Each play is haunted by the specter of the wasted life. Chekhov's characters are caught, however, by life's lesser snares: indecisiveness, loyalty to the wrong cause, and unclarity. The characteristic mood is a sweet, almost aching type of sadness that has come to be known as Chekhovian.
D. A Chekhovian mood is characterized by sweet, almost aching, sadness. The term comes from three dramatic tragedies by Chekhov which revolve around the sadness of a wasted life. The three masterpieces (Uncle Vanya, The Three Sisters, and The Cherry Orchard) share the same

theme and format. The plays are concerned with how the passage of time erodes human aspirations. They are peopled with characters who are struggling with life's lesser problems. These are people who are indecisive, loyal to the wrong causes, or are unable to make themselves clear.

3. I. Movie previews have often helped producers decide which parts of movies they should take out or leave in. 3.____
II. The first 1933 preview of King Kong was very helpful to the producers because many people ran screaming from the theater and would not return when four men first attacked by Kong were eaten by giant spiders.
III. The 1950 premiere of Sunset Boulevard resulted in the filming of an entirely new beginning, and a delay of six months in the film's release.
IV. In the original opening scene, William Holden was in a morgue talking with thirty-six other "corpses" about the ways some of them had died.
V. When he began to tell them of his life with Gloria Swanson, the audience found this hilarious, instead of taking the scene seriously.

A. Movie previews have often helped producers decide what parts of movies they should leave in or take out. For example, the first preview of King Kong in 1933 was very helpful. In one scene, four men were first attacked by Kong and then eaten by giant spiders. Many members of the audience ran screaming from the theater and would not return. The premiere of the 1950 film Sunset Boulevard was also very helpful. In the original opening scene, William Holden was in a morgue with thirty-six other "corpses," discussing the ways some of them had died. When he began to tell them of his life with Gloria Swanson, the audience found this hilarious. They were supposed to take the scene seriously. The result was a delay of six months in the release of the film while a new beginning was added.
B. Movie previews have often helped producers decide whether they should change various parts of a movie. After the 1933 preview of King Kong, a scene in which four men who had been attacked by Kong were eaten by giant spiders was taken out as many people ran screaming from the theater and would not return. The 1950 premiere of Sunset Boulevard also led to some changes. In the original opening scene, William Holden was in a morgue talking with thirty-six other "corpses" about the ways some of them had died. When he began to tell them of his life with Gloria Swanson, the audience found this hilarious, instead of taking the scene seriously.
C. What do Sunset Boulevard and King Kong have in common? Both show the value of using movie previews to test audience reaction. The first 1933 preview of King Kong showed that a scene showing four men being eaten by giant spiders after having been attacked by Kong was too frightening for many people. They ran screaming from the theater and couldn't be coaxed back. The 1950 premiere of Sunset Boulevard was also a scream, but not the kind the producers intended. The movie opens

with William Holden lying in a morgue discussing the ways they had died with thirty-six other "corpses." When he began to tell them of his life with Gloria Swanson, the audience couldn't take him seriously. Their laughter caused a six-month delay while the beginning was rewritten.

D. Producers very often use movie previews to decide if changes are needed. The premiere of Sunset Boulevard in 1950 led to a new beginning and a six-month delay in film release. At the beginning, William Holden and thirty-six other "corpses" discuss the ways some of them died. Rather than taking this seriously, the audience thought it was hilarious when he began to tell them of his life with Gloria Swanson. The first 1933 preview of King Kong was very helpful for its producers because one scene so terrified the audience that many of them ran screaming from the theater and would not return. In this particular scene, four men who had first been attacked by Kong were eaten by giant spiders.

4. I. It is common for supervisors to view employees as "things" to be manipulated. 4.____

II. This approach does not motivate employees, nor does the carrot-and-stick approach because employees often recognize these behaviors and resent them.

III. Supervisors can change these behaviors by using self-inquiry and persistence.

IV. The best managers genuinely respect those they work with, are supportive and helpful, and are interested in working as a team with those they supervise.

V. They disagree with the Golden Rule that says "he or she who has the gold makes the rules."

A. Some managers act as if they think the Golden Rule means "he or she who has the gold makes the rules." They show disrespect to employees by seeing them as "things" to be manipulated. Obviously, this approach does not motivate employees any more than the carrot-and-stick approach motivates them. The employees are smart enough to spot these behaviors and resent them. On the other hand, the managers genuinely respect those they work with, are supportive and helpful, and are interested in working as a team. Self-inquiry and persistence can change even the former type of supervisor into the latter.

B. Many supervisors all into the trap of viewing employees as "things" to be manipulated, or try to motivate them by using a carrot-and-stick approach. These methods do not motivate employees, who often recognize the behaviors and resent them. Supervisors can change these behaviors, however, by using self-inquiry and persistence. The best managers are supportive and helpful, and have genuine respect for those with whom they work. They are interested in working as a team with those they supervise. To them, the Golden Rule is not "he or she who has the gold makes the rules."

C. Some supervisors see employees as "things" to be used or manipulated using a carrot-and-stick technique. These methods don't work. Employees often see through them and resent them. A supervisor who wants to change may do so. The techniques of self-inquiry and persistence can be used to turn him or her into the type of supervisor who doesn't think the Golden Rule is "he or she who has the gold makes the rules." They may become like the best managers who treat those with whom they work with respect and give them help and support. These are the manager who know how to build a team.

D. Unfortunately, many supervisors act as if their employees are objects whose movements they can position at will. This mistaken belief has the same result as another popular motivational technique—the carrot-and-stick approach. Both attitudes can lead to the same result—resentment from those employees who recognize the behaviors for what they are. Supervisors who recognize these behaviors can change through the use of persistence and the use of self-inquiry. It's important to remember that the best managers respect their employees. They readily give necessary help and support and are interested in working as a team with those they supervise. To these managers, the Golden Rule is not "he or she who has the gold makes the rules."

5. I. The first half of the nineteenth century produced a group of pessimistic poets—Byron, De Musset, Heine, Pushkin, and Leopardi. 5.____

II. It also produced a group of pessimistic composers—Schubert, Chopin, Schumann, and even the later Beethoven.

III. Above all, in philosophy, there was the profoundly pessimistic philosopher, Schopenhauer.

IV. The Revolution was dead, the Bourbons were restored, the feudal barons were reclaiming their land, and progress everywhere was being suppressed, as the great age was over.

V. "I thank God," said Goethe, "that I am not young in so thoroughly finished a world."

A. "I thank God," said Goethe, "that I am not young in so thoroughly finished a world." The Revolution was dead, the Bourbons were restored, the feudal barons were reclaiming their land, and progress everywhere was being suppressed. The first half of the nineteenth century produced a group of pessimistic poets: Byron, De Musset, Heine, Pushkin, and Leopardi. It also produced pessimistic composers: Schubert, Chopin, Schumann. Although Beethoven came later, he fits into this group, too. Finally and above all, it also produced a profoundly pessimistic philosopher, Schopenhauer. The great age was over.

B. The first half of the nineteenth century produced a group of pessimistic poets: Byron, De Musset, Heine, Pushkin, and Leopardi. It produced a group of pessimistic composers: Schubert, Chopin, Schumann, and even the later Beethoven. Above all, it produced a profoundly pessimistic philosopher, Schopenhauer. For each of these men, the great age was over. The Revolution was dead, and the Bourbons were restored. The feudal barons were reclaiming their land, and progress everywhere was being suppressed.

C. The great age was over. The Revolution was dead—the Bourbons were restored, and the feudal barons were reclaiming their land. Progress everywhere was being suppressed. Out of this climate came a profound pessimism. Poets, like Byron, De Musset, Heine, Pushkin, and Leopardi; composers, like Schubert, Chopin, Schumann, and even the later Beethoven; and above all, a profoundly pessimistic philosopher, Schopenauer. This pessimism which arose in the first half of the nineteenth century is illustrated by these words of Goethe, "I thank God that I am not young in so thoroughly finished a world."

D. The first half of the nineteenth century produced a group of pessimistic poets, Byron, De Musset, Heine, Pushkin, and Leopardi—and a group of pessimistic composers, Schubert, Chopin, Schumann, and the later Beethoven. Above it all, it produced a profoundly pessimistic philosopher, Schopenhauer. The great age was over. The Revolution was dead, the Bourbons were restored, the feudal barons were reclaiming their land, and progress everywhere was being suppressed. "I thank God," said Goethe, "that I am not young in so thoroughly finished a world."

6. I. A new manager sometimes may feel insecure about his or her competence in the new position. 6.____

II. The new manager may then exhibit defensive or arrogant behavior towards those one supervises, or the new manager may direct overly flattering behavior toward one's new supervisor.

A. Sometimes, a new manager may feel insecure about his or her ability to perform well in this new position. The insecurity may lead him or her to treat others differently. He or she may display arrogant or defensive behavior towards those he or she supervises, or be overly flattering to his or her new supervisor.

B. A new manager may sometimes feel insecure about his or her ability to perform well in the new position. He or she may then become arrogant, defensive, or overly flattering towards those he or she works with.

C. There are times when a new manager may be insecure about how well he or she can perform in the new job. The new manager may also behave defensive or act in an arrogant way towards those he or she supervises, or overly flatter his or her boss.

D. Sometimes a new manager may feel insecure about his or her ability to perform well in the new position. He or she may then display arrogant or defensive behavior towards those they supervise, or become overly flattering towards their supervisors.

7. I. It is possible to eliminate unwanted behavior by bringing it under stimulus control—tying the behavior to a cue, and then never, or rarely, giving the cue. 7.____

II. One trainer successfully used this method to keep an energetic young porpoise from coming out of her tank whenever she felt like it, which was potentially dangerous.

III. Her trainer taught her to do it for a reward, in response to a hand signal, and then rarely gave the signal.

A. Unwanted behavior can be eliminated by tying the behavior to a cue, and then never, or rarely, giving the cue. This is called stimulus control. One trainer was able to use this method to keep an energetic young porpoise from coming out of her tank by teaching her to come out for a reward in response to a hand signal, and then rarely giving the signal.

B. Stimulus control can be used to eliminate unwanted behavior. In this method, behavior is tied to a cue, and then the cue is rarely, if ever, given. One trainer was able to successfully use stimulus control to keep an energetic young porpoise from coming out of her tank whenever she felt like it—a potentially dangerous practice. She taught the porpoise to come out for a reward when she gave a hand signal, and then rarely gave the signal.

C. It is possible to eliminate behavior that is undesirable by bringing it under stimulus control by tying behavior to a signal, and then rarely giving the signal. One trainer successfully used this method to keep an energetic porpoise from coming out of her tank, a potentially dangerous situation. Her trainer taught the porpoise to do it for a reward, in response to a hand signal, and then would rarely give the signal.

D. By using stimulus control, it is possible to eliminate unwanted behavior by tying the behavior to a cue, and then rarely or never give the cue. One trainer was able to use this method to successfully stop a young porpoise from coming out of her tank whenever she felt like it. To curb this potentially dangerous practice, the porpoise was taught by the trainer to come out of the tank for a reward, in response to a hand signal, and then rarely given the signal.

8. I. There is a great deal of concern over the safety of commercial trucks, caused by their greatly increased role in serious accidents since federal deregulation in 1981. 8.____

II. Recently, 60 percent of trucks in New York and Connecticut and 70 percent of trucks in Maryland randomly stopped by state troopers failed safety inspections.

III. Sixteen states in the United States require no training at all for truck drivers.

A. Since federal deregulation in 1981, there has been a great deal of concern over the safety of commercial trucks, and their greatly increased role in serious accidents. Recently, 60 percent of trucks in New York and Connecticut, and 70 percent of trucks in Maryland failed safety inspections. Sixteen states in the United States require no training at all for truck drivers.

B. There is a great deal of concern over the safety of commercial trucks since federal deregulation in 1981. Their role in serious accidents has greatly increased. Recently, 60 percent of trucks randomly stopped in Connecticut and New York and 70 percent in Maryland failed safety inspections conducted by state troopers. Sixteen states in the United States provide no training at all for truck drivers.

C. Commercial trucks have a greatly increased role in serious accidents since federal deregulation in 1981. This has led to a great deal of concern.

Recently, 70 percent of trucks in Maryland and 60 percent of trucks in New York and Connecticut failed inspection of those that were randomly stopped by state troopers. Sixteen states in the United States require no training for all truck drivers.

D. Since federal deregulation in 1981, the role that commercial trucks have played in serious accidents has greatly increased, and this has led to a great deal of concern. Recently, 60 percent of trucks in New York and Connecticut, and 70 percent of trucks in Maryland randomly stopped by state troopers failed safety inspections. Sixteen states in the U.S. don't require any training for truck drivers.

9. I. No matter how much some people have, they still feel unsatisfied and want more, or want to keep what they have forever. 9.____

II. One recent television documentary showed several people flying from New York to Paris for a one-day shopping spree to buy platinum earrings, because they were bored.

III. In Brazil, some people were ordering coffins that cost a minimum of $45,000 and are equipping them with deluxe stereos, televisions, and other graveyard necessities.

A. Some people, despite having a great deal, still feel unsatisfied and want more, or think they can keep what they have forever. One recent documentary on television showed several people enroute from Paris to New York for a one day shopping spree to buy platinum earrings, because they were bored. Some people in Brazil are even ordering coffins equipped with such graveyard necessities as deluxe stereos and televisions. The price of the coffins start at $45,000.

B. No matter how much some people have, they may feel unsatisfied. This leads them to want more, or to want to keep what they have forever. Recently, a television documentary depicting several people flying from New York to Paris for a one day shopping spree to buy platinum earrings. They were bored. Some people in Brazil are ordering coffins that cost at least $45,000 and come equipped with deluxe televisions, stereos and other necessary graveyard items.

C. Some people will be dissatisfied no matter how much they have. They may want more, or they may want to keep what they have forever. One recent television documentary showed several people, motivated by boredom, jetting from New York to Paris for a one-day shopping spree to buy platinum earrings. In Brazil, some people are ordering coffins equipped with deluxe stereos, televisions and other graveyard necessities. The minimum price for these coffins—$45,000.

D. Some people are never satisfied. No matter how much they have they still want more, or think they can keep what they have forever. One television documentary recently showed several people flying from New York to Paris for the day to buy platinum earrings because they were bored. In Brazil, some people are ordering coffins that cost $45,000 and are equipped with deluxe stereos, televisions and other graveyard necessities.

10. I. A television signal or video signal has three parts. 10.____
II. Its parts are the black-and-white portion, the color portion, and the synchronizing (sync) pulses, which keep the picture stable.
III. Each video source, whether it's a camera or a video-cassette recorder contains its own generator of these synchronizing pulses to accompany the picture that it's sending in order to keep it steady and straight.
IV. In order to produce a clean recording, a video-cassette recorder must "lock-up" to the sync pulses that are part of the video it is trying to record, and this effort may be very noticeable if the device does not have gunlock.

A. There are three parts to a television or video signal: the black-and-white part, the color part, and the synchronizing (sync) pulses, which keep the picture stable. Whether it's a video-cassette recorder or a camera, each video source contains its own pulse that synchronizes and generates the picture it's sending in order to keep it straight and steady. A video-cassette recorder must "lock up" to the sync pulses that are part of the video it's trying to record. If the device doesn't have gunlock, this effort must be very noticeable.
B. A video signal or television is comprised of three parts: the black-and-white portion, the color portion, and the sync (synchronizing) pulses, which keep the picture stable. Whether it's a camera or a video-cassette recorder, each video source contains its own generator of these synchronizing pulses. These accompany the picture that it's sending in order to keep it straight and steady. A video-cassette recorder must "lock up" to the sync pulses that are part of the video it is trying to record in order to produce a clean recording. This effort may be very noticeable if the device does not have gunlock.
C. There are three parts to a television or video signal: the color portion, the black-and-white portion, and the sync (synchronizing pulses). These keep the picture stable. Each video source, whether it's a video-cassette recorder or a camera, generates these synchronizing pulses accompanying the picture it's sending in order to keep it straight and steady. If a clean recording is to be produced, a video-cassette recorder must store the sync pulses that are part of the video it is trying to record. This effort may not be noticeable if the device does not have gunlock.
D. A television signal or video signal has three parts: the black-and-white portion, the color portion, and the synchronizing (sync) pulses. It's the sync pulses which keep the picture stable, which accompany it and keep it steady and straight. Whether it's a camera or a video-cassette recorder, each video source contains its own generator of these synchronizing pulses. To produce a clean recording, a video-cassette recorder must "lock up" to the sync pulses that are part of the video it is trying to record. If the device does not have gunlock, this effort may be very noticeable.

KEY (CORRECT ANSWERS)

1.	C	6.	A
2.	B	7.	B
3.	A	8.	D
4.	B	9.	C
5.	D	10.	D

RECORD KEEPING

EXAMINATION SECTION

TEST 1

DIRECTIONS: Each question or incomplete statement is followed by several suggested answers or completions. Select the one that BEST answers the question or completes the statement. *PRINT THE LETTER OF THE CORRECT ANSWER IN THE SPACE AT THE RIGHT.*

Questions 1-15.

DIRECTIONS: Questions 1 through 15 are to be answered on the basis of the following list of company names below. Arrange a file alphabetically, word-by-word, disregarding punctuation, conjunctions, and apostrophes. Then answer the questions.

A Bee C Reading Materials
ABCO Parts
A Better Course for Test Preparation
AAA Auto Parts Co.
A-Z Auto Parts, Inc.
Aabar Books
Abbey, Joanne
Boman-Sylvan Law Firm
BMW Autowerks
C Q Service Company
Chappell-Murray, Inc.
E&E Life Insurance
Emcrisco
Gigi Arts
Gordon, Jon & Associates
SOS Plumbing
Schmidt, J.B. Co.

1. Which of these files should appear FIRST? 1.____
   A. ABCO Parts
   B. A Bee C Reading Materials
   C. A Better Course for Test Preparation
   D. AAA Auto Parts Co.

2. Which of these files should appear SECOND? 2.____
   A. A-Z Auto Parts, Inc.
   B. A Bee C Reading Materials
   C. A Better Course for Test Preparation
   D. AAA Auto Parts Co.

3. Which of these files should appear THIRD? 3.____
   A. ABCO Parts
   B. A Bee C Reading Materials
   C. Aabar Books
   D. AAA Auto Parts Co.

4. Which of these files should appear FOURTH? 4.____
   A. Aabar Books
   B. ABCO Parts
   C. Abbey, Joanne
   D. AAA Auto Parts Co.

5. Which of these files should appear LAST? 5.____
   A. Gordon, Jon & Associates
   B. Gigi Arts
   C. Schmidt, J.B. Co.
   D. SOS Plumbing

6. Which of these files should appear between A-Z Auto Parts, Inc. and Abbey, Joanne? 6.____
   A. A Bee C Reading Materials
   B. AAA Auto Parts Co.
   C. ABCO Parts
   D. A Better Course for Test Preparation

7. Which of these files should appear between ABCO Parts and Aabar Books? 7.____
   A. A Bee C Reading Materials
   B. Abbey, Joanne
   C. Aabar Books
   D. A-Z Auto Parts

8. Which of these files should appear between Abbey, Joanne and Boman-Sylvan Law Firm? 8.____
   A. A Better Course for Test Preparation
   B. BMW Autowerks
   C. Chappell-Murray, Inc.
   D. Aabar Books

9. Which of these files should appear between Abbey, Joanne and C Q Service? 9.____
   A. A-Z Auto Parts, Inc.
   B. BMW Autowerks
   C. Choices A and B
   D. Chappell-Murray, Inc.

10. Which of these files should appear between C Q Service Company and Emcrisco? 10.____
    A. Chappell-Murray, Inc.
    B. E&E Life Insurance
    C. Gigi Arts
    D. Choices A and B

11. Which of these files should NOT appear between C Q Service Company and E&E Life Insurance? 11.____
    A. Gordon, Jon & Associates
    B. Emcrisco
    C. Gigi Arts
    D. All of the above

12. Which of these files should appear between Chappell-Murray, Inc. and Gigi Arts? 12.____
    A. C Q Service Inc., E&E Life Insurance, and Emcrisco
    B. Emcrisco, E&E Life Insurance, and Gordon, Jon & Associates
    C. E&E Life Insurance, and Emcrisco
    D. Emcrisco and Gordon, Jon & Associates

13. Which of these files should appear between Gordon, Jon & Associates and SOS Plumbing? 13.____
    A. Gigi Arts
    B. Schmidt,J.B. Co.
    C. Choices A and B
    D. None of the above

14. Each of the choices lists the four files in their proper alphabetical order EXCEPT 14.____
    A. E&E Life Insurance; Gigi Arts; Gordon, Jon & Associates; SOS Plumbing
    B. E&E Life Insurance; Emcrisco; Gigi Arts; SOS Plumbing
    C. Emcrisco; Gordon, Jon & Associates; SOS Plumbing; Schmidt, J.B. Co.
    D. Emcrisco; Gigi Arts; Gordon, Jon & Associates; SOS Plumbing

15. Which of the choices lists the four files in their proper alphabetical order? 15.____
    A. Gigi Arts; Gordon, Jon & Associates; SOS Plumbing; Schmidt, J.B. Co.
    B. Gordon, Jon & Associates; Gigi Arts; Schmidt, J.B. Co.; SOS Plumbing
    C. Gordon, Jon & Associates; Gigi Arts; SOS Plumbing; Schmidt, J.B. Co.
    D. Gigi Arts; Gordon, Jon & Associates; Schmidt, J.B. Co.; SOS Plumbing

16. The alphabetical filing order of two businesses with identical names is determined by the 16.____
    A. length of time each business has been operating
    B. addresses of the businesses
    C. last name of the company president
    D. no one of the above

17. In an alphabetical filing system, if a business name includes a number, it should be 17.____
    A. disregarded
    B. considered a number and placed at the end of an alphabetical section
    C. treated as though it were written in words and alphabetized accordingly
    D. considered a number and placed at the beginning of an alphabetical section

18. If a business name includes a contraction (such as *don't* or *it's*), how should that word be treated in an alphabetical system? 18.____
    A. Divide the word into its separate parts and treat it as two words
    B. Ignore the letters that come after the apostrophe
    C. Ignore the word that contains the contraction
    D. Ignore the apostrophe and consider all letters in the contraction

19. In what order should the parts of an address be considered when using an alphabetical filing system? 19.____
    A. City or town; state; street name; house or building number
    B. State; city or town; street name; house or building number
    C. House or building number; street name; city or town; state
    D. Street name; city or town; state

20. A business record should be cross-referenced when a(n) 20.____
    A. organization is known by an abbreviated name
    B. business has a name change because of a sale, incorporation, or other reason
    C. business is known by a *coined* or common name which differs from a dictionary spelling
    D. all of the above

21. A geographical filing system is MOST effective when 21.____
    A. location is more important than name
    B. many names or titles sound alike
    C. dealing with companies who have offices all over the world
    D. filing personal and business files

Questions 22-25.

DIRECTIONS: Questions 22 through 25 are to be answered on the basis of the list of items below, which are to be filed geographically. Organize the items geographically and then answer the questions.

I. University Press at Berkeley, U.S.
II. Maria Sanchez, Mexico City, Mexico
III. Great Expectations Ltd. in London, England
IV. Justice League, Cape Town, South Africa, Africa
V. Crown Pearls Ltd. in London, England
VI. Joseph Prasad in London, England

22. Which of the following arrangements of the items is composed according to the policy of: *Continent, Country, City, Firm or Individual Name*? 22.____
    A. V, III, IV, VI, II, I
    B. IV, V, III, VI, II, I
    C. I, IV, V, III, VI, II
    D. IV, V, III, VI, I, II

23. Which of the following files is arranged according to the policy of: *Continent, Country, City, Firm or Individual Name*? 23.____
    A. South Africa; Africa; Cape Town; Justice League
    B. Mexico; Mexico City; Maria Sanchez
    C. North America; United States; Berkeley; University Press
    D. England; Europe; London; Prasad, Joseph

24. Which of the following arrangements of the items is composed according to the policy of: *Country, City, Firm or Individual Name*? 24.____
    A. V, VI, III, II, IV, I
    B. I, V, VI, III, II, IV
    C. VI, V, III, II, IV, I
    D. V, III, VI, II, IV, I

25. Which of the following files is arranged according to a policy of: *Country, City, Firm or Individual Name*? 25.____
    A. England; London; Crown Pearls Ltd.
    B. North America; United States; Berkeley; University Press
    C. Africa; Cape Town; Justice League
    D. Mexico City; Mexico; Maria Sanchez

26. Under which of the following circumstances would a phonetic filing system be MOST effective? 26.____
    A. When the person in charge of filing can't spell very well
    B. With large files with names that sound alike
    C. With large files with names that are spelled alike
    D. All of the above

Questions 27-29.

DIRECTIONS: Questions 27 through 29 are to be answered on the basis of the following list of numerical files.

I. 391-023-100
II. 361-132-170
III. 385-732-200
IV. 381-432-150
V. 391-632-387
VI. 361-423-303
VII. 391-123-271

27. Which of the following arrangements of the files follows a consecutive-digit system? 27.____
    A. II, III, IV, I
    B. I, V, VII, III
    C. II, IV, III, I
    D. III, I, V, VII

28. Which of the following arrangements follows a terminal-digit system? 28.____
    A. I, VII, II, IV, III
    B. II, I, IV, V, VII
    C. VII, VI, V, IV, III
    D. I, IV, II, III, VII

29. Which of the following lists follows a middle-digit system? 29.____
    A. I, VII, II, VI, IV, V, III
    B. I, II, VII, IV, VI, V, III
    C. VII, II, I, III, V, VI, IV
    D. VII, I, II, IV, VI, V, III

Questions 30-31.

DIRECTIONS: Questions 30 and 31 are to be answered on the basis of the following information.

I. Reconfirm Laura Bates appointment with James Caldecort on December 12 at 9:30 A.M.
II. Laurence Kinder contact Julia Lucas on August 3 and set up a meeting for week of September 23 at 4 P.M.
III. John Lutz contact Larry Waverly on August 3 and set up appointment for September 23 at 9:30 A.M.
IV. Call for tickets for Gerry Stanton August 21 for New Jersey on September 23, flight 143 at 4:43 P.M.

30. A chronological file for the above information would be 30.____
A. IV, III, II, I B. III, II, IV, I C. IV, II, III, I D. III, I, II, IV

31. Using the above information, a chronological file for the date September 23 would be 31.____
A. II, III, IV B. III, I, IV C. III, II, IV D. IV, III, II

Questions 32-34.

DIRECTIONS: Questions 32 through 34 are to be answered on the basis of the following information.

I. Call Roger Epstein, Ashoke Naipaul, Jon Anderson, and Sara Washingon on April 19 at 1:00 P.M. to set up meeting with Alika D'Ornay for June 6 in New York.
II. Call Martin Ames before noon on April 19 to confirm afternoon meeting with Bob Greenwood on April 20th.
III. Set up meeting room at noon for 2:30 P.M. meeting on April 19th.
IV. Ashley Stanton contact Bob Greenwood at 9:00 A.M. on April 20 and set up meeting for June 6 at 8:30 A.M.
V. Carol Guiland contact Shelby Van Ness during afternoon of April 20 and set up meeting for June 6 at 10:00 A.M.
VI. Call airline and reserve tickets on June 6 for Roger Epstein trip to Denver on July 8.
VII. Meeting at 2:30 P.M. on April 19th.

32. A chronological file for all of the above information would be 32.____
A. II, I, III, VII, V, IV, VI B. III, VII, II, I, IV, V, VI
C. III, VII, I, II, V, IV, VI D. II, III, I, VII, IV, V, VI

33. A chronological file for the date of April 19th would be 33.____
A. II, III, VII, I B. II, III, I, VII C. VII, I, III, II D. III, VII, I, II

34. Add the following information to the file, and then create a chronological file for April 20th: VIII. April 20: 3:00 P.M. meeting between Bob Greenwood and Martin Ames. 34.____
   A. IV, V, VIII B. IV, VIII, V C. VIII, V, IV D. V, IV, VIII

35. The PRIMARY advantage of computer records over a manual system is 35.____
   A. speed of retrieval
   B. accuracy
   C. cost
   D. potential file loss

KEY (CORRECT ANSWERS)

1.	B	11.	D	21.	A	31.	C
2.	C	12.	C	22.	B	32.	D
3.	D	13.	B	23.	C	33.	B
4.	A	14.	C	24.	D	34.	A
5.	D	15.	D	25.	A	35.	A
6.	C	16.	B	26.	B		
7.	B	17.	C	27.	C		
8.	B	18.	D	28.	D		
9.	C	19.	A	29.	A		
10.	D	20.	D	30.	B		

PHILOSOPHY, PRINCIPLES, PRACTICES, AND TECHNICS OF SUPERVISION, ADMINISTRATION, MANAGEMENT, AND ORGANIZATION

TABLE OF CONTENTS

PHILOSOPHY, PRINCIPLES, PRACTICES, AND TECHNICS
OF
SUPERVISION, ADMINISTRATION, MANAGEMENT, AND ORGANIZATION

MEANING OF SUPERVISION

The extension of the democratic philosophy has been accompanied by an extension in the scope of supervision. Modern leaders and supervisors no longer think of supervision in the narrow sense of being confined chiefly to visiting employees, supplying materials, or rating the staff. They regard supervision as being intimately related to all the concerned agencies of society, they speak of the supervisor's function in terms of "growth," rather than the "improvement" of employees.

This modern concept of supervision may be defined as follows: Supervision is leadership and the development of leadership within groups which are cooperatively engaged in inspection, research, training, guidance, and evaluation.

THE OLD AND THE NEW SUPERVISION

TRADITIONAL
1. Inspection
2. Focused on the employee
3. Visitation
4. Random and haphazard
5. Imposed and authoritarian
6. One person usually

MODERN
1. Study and analysis
2. Focused on aims, materials, methods, supervisors, employees, environment
3. Demonstrations, intervisitation, workshops, directed reading, bulletins, etc.
4. Definitely organized and planned (scientific)
5. Cooperative and democratic
6. Many persons involved (creative)

THE EIGHT (8) BASIC PRINCIPLES OF THE NEW SUPERVISION

I. Principle of Responsibility
Authority to act and responsibility for acting must be joined.
A. If you give responsibility, give authority.
B. Define employee duties clearly.
C. Protect employees from criticism by others.
D. Recognize the rights as well as obligations of employees.
E. Achieve the aims of a democratic society insofar as it is possible within the area of your work.
F. Establish a situation favorable to training and learning.
G. Accept ultimate responsibility for everything done in your section, unit, office, division, department.
H. Good administration and good supervision are inseparable.

II. Principle of Authority

The success of the supervisor is measured by the extent to which the power of authority is not used.

A. Exercise simplicity and informality in supervision
B. Use the simplest machinery of supervision
C. If it is good for the organization as a whole, it is probably justified.
D. Seldom be arbitrary or authoritative.
E. Do not base your work on the power of position or of personality.
F. Permit and encourage the free expression of opinions.

III. Principle of Self-Growth

The success of the supervisor is measured by the extent to which, and the speed with which, he is no longer needed.

A. Base criticism on principles, not on specifics.
B. Point out higher activities to employees.
C. Train for self-thinking by employees to meet new situations.
D. Stimulate initiative, self-reliance, and individual responsibility
E. Concentrate on stimulating the growth of employees rather than on removing defects.

IV. Principle of Individual Worth

Respect for the individual is a paramount consideration in supervision.

A. Be human and sympathetic in dealing with employees.
B. Don't nag about things to be done.
C. Recognize the individual differences among employees and seek opportunities to permit best expression of each personality.

V. Principle of Creative Leadership

The best supervision is that which is not apparent to the employee.

A. Stimulate, don't drive employees to creative action.
B. Emphasize doing good things.
C. Encourage employees to do what they do best.
D. Do not be too greatly concerned with details of subject or method.
E. Do not be concerned exclusively with immediate problems and activities.
F. Reveal higher activities and make them both desired and maximally possible.
G. Determine procedures in the light of each situation but see that these are derived from a sound basic philosophy.
H. Aid, inspire, and lead so as to liberate the creative spirit latent in all good employees.

VI. Principle of Success and Failure

There are no unsuccessful employees, only unsuccessful supervisors who have failed to give proper leadership.

A. Adapt suggestions to the capacities, attitudes, and prejudices of employees.
B. Be gradual, be progressive, be persistent.
C. Help the employee find the general principle; have the employee apply his own problem to the general principle.
D. Give adequate appreciation for good work and honest effort.
E. Anticipate employee difficulties and help to prevent them.
F. Encourage employees to do the desirable things they will do anyway.
G. Judge your supervision by the results it secures.

VII. Principle of Science
Successful supervision is scientific, objective, and experimental. It is based on facts, not on prejudices.
A. Be cumulative in results.
B. Never divorce your suggestions from the goals of training.
C. Don't be impatient of results.
D. Keep all matters on a professional, not a personal, level.
E. Do not be concerned exclusively with immediate problems and activities.
F. Use objective means of determining achievement and rating where possible.

VIII. Principle of Cooperation
Supervision is a cooperative enterprise between supervisor and employee.
A. Begin with conditions as they are.
B. Ask opinions of all involved when formulating policies.
C. Organization is as good as its weakest link.
D. Let employees help to determine policies and department programs.
E. Be approachable and accessible—physically and mentally.
F. Develop pleasant social relationships.

WHAT IS ADMINISTRATION

Administration is concerned with providing the environment, the material facilities, and the operational procedures that will promote the maximum growth and development of supervisors and employees. (Organization is an aspect and a concomitant of administration.)

There is no sharp line of demarcation between supervision and administration; these functions are intimately interrelated and, often, overlapping. They are complementary activities.

I. Practices Commonly Classed as "Supervisory"
A. Conducting employees' conferences
B. Visiting sections, units, offices, divisions, departments
C. Arranging for demonstrations
D. Examining plans
E. Suggesting professional reading
F. Interpreting bulletins
G. Recommending in-service training courses
H. Encouraging experimentation
I. Appraising employee morale
J. Providing for intervisitation

II. Practices Commonly Classified as "Administrative"
A. Management of the office
B. Arrangement of schedules for extra duties
C. Assignment of rooms or areas
D. Distribution of supplies
E. Keeping records and reports
F. Care of audio-visual materials
G. Keeping inventory records
H. Checking record cards and books

I. Programming special activities
J. Checking on the attendance and punctuality of employees

III. Practices Commonly Classified as Both "Supervisory" and "Administrative"
   A. Program construction
   B. Testing or evaluating outcomes
   C. Personnel accounting
   D. Ordering instructional materials

RESPONSIBILITIES OF THE SUPERVISOR

A person employed in a supervisory capacity must constantly be able to improve his own efficiency and ability. He represent the employer to the employees and only continuous self-examination can make him a capable supervisor.

Leadership and training are the supervisor's responsibility. An efficient working unit is one in which the employees work with the supervisor. It is his job to bring out the best in his employees. He must always be relaxed, courteous, and calm in his association with his employees. Their feelings are important, and a harsh attitude does not develop the most efficient employees.

COMPETENCES OF THE SUPERVISOR

I. Complete knowledge of the duties and responsibilities of his position.
II. To be able to organize a job, plan ahead, and carry through.
III. To have self-confidence and initiative.
IV. To be able to handle the unexpected situation and make quick decisions.
V. To be able to properly train subordinates in the positions they are best suited for.
VI. To be able to keep good human relations among his subordinates.
VII. To be able to keep good human relations between his subordinates and himself and to earn their respect and trust.

THE PROFESSIONAL SUPERVISOR-EMPLOYEE RELATIONSHIP

There are two kinds of efficiency: one kind is only apparent and is produced in organizations through the exercise of mere discipline; this is but a simulation of the second, or true, efficiency which springs from spontaneous cooperation. If you are a manager, no matter how great or small your responsibility, it is your job, in the final analysis, to create and develop this involuntary cooperation among the people whom you supervise. For, no matter how powerful a combination of money, machines, and materials a company may have, this is a dead and sterile thing without a team of willing, thinking, and articulate people to guide it.

The following 21 points are presented as indicative of the exemplary basic relationship that should exist between supervisor and employee:

1. Each person wants to be liked and respected by his fellow employee and wants to be treated with consideration and respect by his superior.
2. The most competent employee will make an error. However, in a unit where good relations exist between the supervisor and his employees, tenseness and fear do not exist. Thus, errors are not hidden or covered up, and the efficiency of a unit is not impaired.

3. Subordinates resent rules, regulations, or orders that are unreasonable or unexplained.
4. Subordinates are quick to resent unfairness, harshness, injustices, and favoritism.
5. An employee will accept responsibility if he knows that he will be complimented for a job well done, and not too harshly chastised for failure; that his supervisor will check the cause of the failure, and, if it was the supervisor's fault, he will assume the blame therefore. If it was the employee's fault, his supervisor will explain the correct method or means of handling the responsibility.
6. An employee wants to receive credit for a suggestion he has made, that is used. If a suggestion cannot be used, the employee is entitled to an explanation. The supervisor should not say "no" and close the subject.
7. Fear and worry slow up a worker's ability. Poor working environment can impair his physical and mental health. A good supervisor avoids forceful methods, threats, and arguments to get a job done.
8. A forceful supervisor is able to train his employees individually and as a team, and is able to motivate them in the proper channels.
9. A mature supervisor is able to properly evaluate his subordinates and to keep them happy and satisfied.
10. A sensitive supervisor will never patronize his subordinates.
11. A worthy supervisor will respect his employees' confidences.
12. Definite and clear-cut responsibilities should be assigned to each executive.
13. Responsibility should always be coupled with corresponding authority.
14. No change should be made in the scope or responsibilities of a position without a definite understanding to that effect on the part of all persons concerned.
15. No executive or employee, occupying a single position in the organization, should be subject to definite orders from more than one source.
16. Orders should never be given to subordinates over the head of a responsible executive. Rather than do this, the officer in question should be supplanted.
17. Criticisms of subordinates should, whoever possible, be made privately, and in no case should a subordinate be criticized in the presence of executives or employees of equal or lower rank.
18. No dispute or difference between executives or employees as to authority or responsibilities should be considered too trivial for prompt and careful adjudication.
19. Promotions, wage changes, and disciplinary action should always be approved by the executive immediately superior to the one directly responsible.
20. No executive or employee should ever be required, or expected, to be at the same time an assistant to, and critic of, another.
21. Any executive whose work is subject to regular inspection should, wherever practicable, be given the assistance and facilities necessary to enable him to maintain an independent check of the quality of his work.

MINI-TEXT IN SUPERVISION, ADMINISTRATION, MANAGEMENT, AND ORGANIZATION

I. Brief Highlights

Listed concisely and sequentially are major headings and important data in the field for quick recall and review.

A. Levels of Management

Any organization of some size has several levels of management. In terms of a ladder, the levels are:

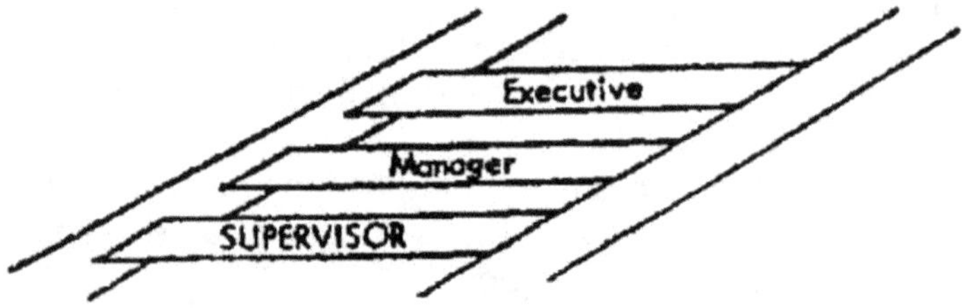

The first level is very important because it is the beginning point of management leadership.

B. What the Supervisor Must Learn

A supervisor must learn to:

1. Deal with people and their differences
2. Get the job done through people
3. Recognize the problems when they exist
4. Overcome obstacles to good performance
5. Evaluate the performance of people
6. Check his own performance in terms of accomplishment

C. A Definition of Supervisor

The term supervisor means any individual having authority, in the interests of the employer, to hire, transfer, suspend, lay-off, recall, promote, discharge, assign, reward, or discipline other employees or responsibility to direct them, or to adjust their grievances, or effectively to recommend such action, if, in connection with the foregoing, exercise of such authority is not of a merely routine or clerical nature but requires the use of independent judgment.

D. Elements of the Team Concept

What is involved in teamwork? The component parts are:

1. Members
2. A leader
3. Goals
4. Plans
5. Cooperation
6. Spirit

E. Principles of Organization

1. A team member must know what his job is.
2. Be sure that the nature and scope of a job are understood.
3. Authority and responsibility should be carefully spelled out.
4. A supervisor should be permitted to make the maximum number of decisions affecting his employees.
5. Employees should report to only one supervisor.
6. A supervisor should direct only as many employees as he can handle effectively.
7. An organization plan should be flexible.

8. Inspection and performance of work should be separate.
9. Organizational problems should receive immediate attention.
10. Assign work in line with ability and experience.

F. The Four Important Parts of Every Job
1. Inherent in every job is the *accountability* for results.
2. A second set of factors in every job is *responsibilities*.
3. Along with duties and responsibilities one must have the *authority* to act within certain limits without obtaining permission to proceed.
4. No job exists in a vacuum. The supervisor is surrounded by key *relationships*.

G. Principles of Delegation
Where work is delegated for the first time, the supervisor should think in terms of these questions:
1. Who is best qualified to do this?
2. Can an employee improve his abilities by doing this?
3. How long should an employee spend on this?
4. Are there any special problems for which he will need guidance?
5. How broad a delegation can I make?

H. Principles of Effective Communications
1. Determine the media.
2. To whom directed?
3. Identification and source authority.
4. Is communication understood?

I. Principles of Work Improvement
1. Most people usually do only the work which is assigned to them.
2. Workers are likely to fit assigned work into the time available to perform it.
3. A good workload usually stimulates output.
4. People usually do their best work when they know that results will be reviewed or inspected.
5. Employees usually feel that someone else is responsible for conditions of work, workplace layout, job methods, type of tools/equipment, and other such factors.
6. Employees are usually defensive about their job security.
7. Employees have natural resistance to change.
8. Employees can support or destroy a supervisor.
9. A supervisor usually earns the respect of his people through his personal example of diligence and efficiency.

J. Areas of Job Improvement
The areas of job improvement are quite numerous, but the most common ones which a supervisor can identify and utilize are:
1. Departmental layout
2. Flow of work
3. Workplace layout
4. Utilization of manpower
5. Work methods
6. Materials handling

7. Utilization
8. Motion economy

K. Seven Key Points in Making Improvements
1. Select the job to be improved
2. Study how it is being done now
3. Question the present method
4. Determine actions to be taken
5. Chart proposed method
6. Get approval and apply
7. Solicit worker participation

I. Corrective Techniques of Job Improvement

Specific Problems
1. Size of workload
2. Inability to meet schedules
3. Strain and fatigue
4. Improper use of men and skills
5. Waste, poor quality, unsafe conditions
6. Bottleneck conditions that hinder output
7. Poor utilization of equipment and machine
8. Efficiency and productivity of labor

General Improvement
1. Departmental layout
2. Flow of work
3. Work plan layout
4. Utilization of manpower
5. Work methods
6. Materials handling
7. Utilization of equipment
8. Motion economy

Corrective Techniques
1. Study with scale model
2. Flow chart study
3. Motion analysis
4. Comparison of units produced to standard allowance
5. Methods analysis
6. Flow chart and equipment study
7. Down time vs. running time
8. Motion analysis

M. A Planning Checklist
1. Objectives
2. Controls
3. Delegations
4. Communications
5. Resources
6. Manpower

7. Equipment
8. Supplies and materials
9. Utilization of time
10. Safety
11. Money
12. Work
13. Timing of improvements

N. Five Characteristics of Good Directions

In order to get results, directions must be:

1. Possible of accomplishment
2. Agreeable with worker interests
3. Related to mission
4. Planned and complete
5. Unmistakably clear

O. Types of Directions

1. Demands or direct orders
2. Requests
3. Suggestion or implication
4. volunteering

P. Controls

A typical listing of the overall areas in which the supervisor should establish controls might be:

1. Manpower
2. Materials
3. Quality of work
4. Quantity of work
5. Time
6. Space
7. Money
8. Methods

Q. Orienting the New Employee

1. Prepare for him
2. Welcome the new employee
3. Orientation for the job
4. Follow-up

R. Checklist for Orienting New Employees

	Yes	No
1. Do you appreciate the feelings of new employees when they first report for work?	___	___
2. Are you aware of the fact that the new employee must make a big adjustment to his job?	___	___
3. Have you given him good reasons for liking the job and the organization?	___	___
4. Have you prepared for his first day on the job?	___	___
5. Did you welcome him cordially and make him feel needed?	___	___

	Yes	No
6. Did you establish rapport with him so that he feels free to talk and discuss matters with you?	___	___
7. Did you explain his job to him and his relationship to you?	___	___
8. Does he know that his work will be evaluated periodically on a basis that is fair and objective?	___	___
9. Did you introduce him to his fellow workers in such a way that they are likely to accept him?	___	___
10. Does he know what employee benefits he will receive?	___	___
11. Does he understand the importance of being on the job and what to do if he must leave his duty station?	___	___
12. Has he been impressed with the importance of accident prevention and safe practice?	___	___
13. Does he generally know his way around the department?	___	___
14. Is he under the guidance of a sponsor who will teach the right way of doing things?	___	___
15. Do you plan to follow-up so that he will continue to adjust successfully to his job?	___	___

S. Principles of Learning
1. Motivation
2. Demonstration or explanation
3. Practice

T. Causes of Poor Performance
1. Improper training for job
2. Wrong tools
3. Inadequate directions
4. Lack of supervisory follow-up
5. Poor communications
6. Lack of standards of performance
7. Wrong work habits
8. Low morale
9. Other

U. Four Major Steps in On-The-Job Instruction
1. Prepare the worker
2. Present the operation
3. Tryout performance
4. Follow-up

V. Employees Want Five Things
1. Security
2. Opportunity
3. Recognition
4. Inclusion
5. Expression

W. Some Don'ts in Regard to Praise
1. Don't praise a person for something he hasn't done.
2. Don't praise a person unless you can be sincere.
3. Don't be sparing in praise just because your superior withholds it from you.
4. Don't let too much time elapse between good performance and recognition of it

X. How to Gain Your Workers' Confidence
Methods of developing confidence include such things as:
1. Knowing the interests, habits, hobbies of employees
2. Admitting your own inadequacies
3. Sharing and telling of confidence in others
4. Supporting people when they are in trouble
5. Delegating matters that can be well handled
6. Being frank and straightforward about problems and working conditions
7. Encouraging others to bring their problems to you
8. Taking action on problems which impede worker progress

Y. Sources of Employee Problems
On-the-job causes might be such things as:
1. A feeling that favoritism is exercised in assignments
2. Assignment of overtime
3. An undue amount of supervision
4. Changing methods or systems
5. Stealing of ideas or trade secrets
6. Lack of interest in job
7. Threat of reduction in force
8. Ignorance or lack of communications
9. Poor equipment
10. Lack of knowing how supervisor feels toward employee
11. Shift assignments

Off-the-job problems might have to do with:
1. Health
2. Finances
3. Housing
4. Family

Z. The Supervisor's Key to Discipline
There are several key points about discipline which the supervisor should keep in mind:
1. Job discipline is one of the disciplines of life and is directed by the supervisor.
2. It is more important to correct an employee fault than to fix blame for it.
3. Employee performance is affected by problems both on the job and off.
4. Sudden or abrupt changes in behavior can be indications of important employee problems.
5. Problems should be dealt with as soon as possible after they are identified.
6. The attitude of the supervisor may have more to do with solving problems than the techniques of problem solving.
7. Correction of employee behavior should be resorted to only after the supervisor is sure that training or counseling will not be helpful.

8. Be sure to document your disciplinary actions.
9. Make sure that you are disciplining on the basis of facts rather than personal feelings.
10. Take each disciplinary step in order, being careful not to make snap judgments, or decisions based on impatience.

AA. Five Important Processes of Management
1. Planning
2. Organizing
3. Scheduling
4. Controlling
5. Motivating

BB. When the Supervisor Fails to Plan
1. Supervisor creates impression of not knowing his job
2. May lead to excessive overtime
3. Job runs itself—supervisor lacks control
4. Deadlines and appointments missed
5. Parts of the work go undone
6. Work interrupted by emergencies
7. Sets a bad example
8. Uneven workload creates peaks and valleys
9. Too much time on minor details at expense of more important tasks

CC. Fourteen General Principles of Management
1. Division of work
2. Authority and responsibility
3. Discipline
4. Unity of command
5. Unity of direction
6. Subordination of individual interest to general interest
7. Remuneration of personnel
8. Centralization
9. Scalar chain
10. Order
11. Equity
12. Stability of tenure of personnel
13. Initiative
14. Esprit de corps

DD. Change

Bringing about change is perhaps attempted more often, and yet less well understood, than anything else the supervisor does. How do people generally react to change? (People tend to resist change that is imposed upon them by other individuals or circumstances.

Change is characteristic of every situation. It is a part of every real endeavor where the efforts of people are concerned.

1. Why do people resist change?
   People may resist change because of:
   a. Fear of the unknown
   b. Implied criticism
   c. Unpleasant experiences in the past
   d. Fear of loss of status
   e. Threat to the ego
   f. Fear of loss of economic stability

2. How can we best overcome the resistance to change?
   In initiating change, take these steps:
   a. Get ready to sell
   b. Identify sources of help
   c. Anticipate objections
   d. Sell benefits
   e. Listen in depth
   f. Follow up

II. Brief Topical Summaries

A. Who/What is the Supervisor?
1. The supervisor is often called the "highest level employee and the lowest level manager."
2. A supervisor is a member of both management and the work group. He acts as a bridge between the two.
3. Most problems in supervision are in the area of human relations, or people problems.
4. Employees expect: Respect, opportunity to learn and to advance, and a sense of belonging, and so forth.
5. Supervisors are responsible for directing people and organizing work. Planning is of paramount importance.
6. A position description is a set of duties and responsibilities inherent to a given position.
7. It is important to keep the position description up-to-date and to provide each employee with his own copy.

B. The Sociology of Work
1. People are alike in many ways; however, each individual is unique.
2. The supervisor is challenged in getting to know employee differences. Acquiring skills in evaluating individuals is an asset.
3. Maintaining meaningful working relationships in the organization is of great importance.
4. The supervisor has an obligation to help individuals to develop to their fullest potential.
5. Job rotation on a planned basis helps to build versatility and to maintain interest and enthusiasm in work groups.
6. Cross training (job rotation) provides backup skills.

7. The supervisor can help reduce tension by maintaining a sense of humor, providing guidance to employees, and by making reasonable and timely decisions. Employees respond favorably to working under reasonably predictable circumstances.
8. Change is characteristic of all managerial behavior. The supervisor must adjust to changes in procedures, new methods, technological changes, and to a number of new and sometimes challenging situations.
9. To overcome the natural tendency for people to resist change, the supervisor should become more skillful in initiating change.

C. Principles and Practices of Supervision

1. Employees should be required to answer to only one superior.
2. A supervisor can effectively direct only a limited number of employees, depending upon the complexity, variety, and proximity of the jobs involved.
3. The organizational chart presents the organization in graphic form. It reflects lines of authority and responsibility as well as interrelationships of units within the organization.
4. Distribution of work can be improved through an analysis using the "Work Distribution Chart."
5. The "Work Distribution Chart" reflects the division of work within a unit in understandable form.
6. When related tasks are given to an employee, he has a better chance of increasing his skills through training.
7. The individual who is given the responsibility for tasks must also be given the appropriate authority to insure adequate results.
8. The supervisor should delegate repetitive, routine work. Preparation of recurring reports, maintaining leave and attendance records are some examples.
9. Good discipline is essential to good task performance. Discipline is reflected in the actions of employees on the job in the absence of supervision.
10. Disciplinary action may have to be taken when the positive aspects of discipline have failed. Reprimand, warning, and suspension are examples of disciplinary action.
11. If a situation calls for a reprimand, be sure it is deserved and remember it is to be done in private.

D. Dynamic Leadership

1. A style is a personal method or manner of exerting influence.
2. Authoritarian leaders often see themselves as the source of power and authority.
3. The democratic leader often perceives the group as the source of authority and power.
4. Supervisors tend to do better when using the pattern of leadership that is most natural for them.
5. Social scientists suggest that the effective supervisor use the leadership style that best fits the problem or circumstances involved.
6. All four styles—telling, selling, consulting, joining—have their place. Using one does not preclude using the other at another time.

7. The theory X point of view assumes that the average person dislikes work, will avoid it whenever possible, and must be coerced to achieve organizational objectives.
8. The theory Y point of view assumes that the average person considers work to be a natural as play, and, when the individual is committed, he requires little supervision or direction to accomplish desired objectives.
9. The leader's basic assumptions concerning human behavior and human nature affect his actions, decisions, and other managerial practices.
10. Dissatisfaction among employees is often present, but difficult to isolate. The supervisor should seek to weaken dissatisfaction by keeping promises, being sincere and considerate, keeping employees informed, and so forth.
11. Constructive suggestions should be encouraged during the natural progress of the work.

E. Processes for Solving Problems

1. People find their daily tasks more meaningful and satisfying when they can improve them.
2. The causes of problems, or the key factors, are often hidden in the background. Ability to solve problems often involves the ability to isolate them from their backgrounds. There is some substance to the cliché that some persons "can't see the forest for the trees."
3. New procedures are often developed from old ones. Problems should be broken down into manageable parts. New ideas can be adapted from old one.
4. People think differently in problem-solving situations. Using a logical, patterned approach is often useful. One approach found to be useful includes these steps:
   a. Define the problem
   b. Establish objectives
   c. Get the facts
   d. Weigh and decide
   e. Take action
   f. Evaluate action

F. Training for Results

1. Participants respond best when they feel training is important to them.
2. The supervisor has responsibility for the training and development of those who report to him.
3. When training is delegated to others, great care must be exercised to insure the trainer has knowledge, aptitude, and interest for his work as a trainer.
4. Training (learning) of some type goes on continually. The most successful supervisor makes certain the learning contributes in a productive manner to operational goals.
5. New employees are particularly susceptible to training. Older employees facing new job situations require specific training, as well as having need for development and growth opportunities.
6. Training needs require continuous monitoring.
7. The training officer of an agency is a professional with a responsibility to assist supervisors in solving training problems.

8. Many of the self-development steps important to the supervisor's own growth are equally important to the development of peers and subordinates. Knowledge of these is important when the supervisor consults with others on development and growth opportunities.

G. Health, Safety, and Accident Prevention
1. Management-minded supervisors take appropriate measures to assist employees in maintaining health and in assuring safe practices in the work environment.
2. Effective safety training and practices help to avoid injury and accidents.
3. Safety should be a management goal. All infractions of safety which are observed should be corrected without exception.
4. Employees' safety attitude, training and instruction, provision of safe tools and equipment, supervision, and leadership are considered highly important factors which contribute to safety and which can be influenced directly by supervisors.
5. When accidents do occur, they should be investigated promptly for very important reasons, including the fact that information which is gained can be used to prevent accidents in the future.

H. Equal Employment Opportunity
1. The supervisor should endeavor to treat all employees fairly, without regard to religion, race, sex, or national origin.
2. Groups tend to reflect the attitude of the leader. Prejudice can be detected even in very subtle form. Supervisors must strive to create a feeling of mutual respect and confidence in every employee.
3. Complete utilization of all human resources is a national goal. Equitable consideration should be accorded women in the work force, minority-group members, the physically and mentally handicapped, and the older employee. The important question is: "Who can do the job?"
4. Training opportunities, recognition for performance, overtime assignments, promotional opportunities, and all other personnel actions are to be handled on an equitable basis.

I. Improving Communications
1. Communications is achieving understanding between the sender and the receiver of a message. It also means sharing information—the creation of understanding.
2. Communication is basic to all human activity. Words are means of conveying meanings; however, real meanings are in people.
3. There are very practical differences in the effectiveness of one-way, impersonal, and two-way communications. Words spoken face-to-face are better understood. Telephone conversations are effective, but lack the rapport of person-to-person exchanges. The whole person communicates.
4. Cooperation and communication in an organization go hand in hand. When there is a mutual respect between people, spelling out rules and procedures for communicating is unnecessary.
5. There are several barriers to effective communications. These include failure to listen with respect and understanding, lack of skill in feedback, and misinterpreting the meanings of words used by the speaker. It is also common

practice to listen to what we want to hear, and tune out things we do not want to hear.

6. Communication is management's chief problem. The supervisor should accept the challenge to communicate more effectively and to improve interagency and intra-agency communications.
7. The supervisor may often plan for and conduct meetings. The planning phase is critical and may determine the success or the failure of a meeting.
8. Speaking before groups usually requires extra effort. Stage fright may never disappear completely, but it can be controlled.

J. Self-Development
1. Every employee is responsible for his own self-development.
2. Toastmaster and toastmistress clubs offer opportunities to improve skills in oral communications.
3. Planning for one's own self-development is of vital importance. Supervisors know their own strengths and limitations better than anyone else.
4. Many opportunities are open to aid the supervisor in his developmental efforts, including job assignments; training opportunities, both governmental and non-governmental—to include universities and professional conferences and seminars.
5. Programmed instruction offers a means of studying at one's own rate.
6. Where difficulties may arise from a supervisor's being away from his work for training, he may participate in televised home study or correspondence courses to meet his self-development needs.

K. Teaching and Training
1. The Teaching Process
Teaching is encouraging and guiding the learning activities of students toward established goals. In most cases this process consists of five steps: preparation, presentation, summarization, evaluation, and application.

a. Preparation
Preparation is two-fold in nature; that of the supervisor and the employee. Preparation by the supervisor is absolutely essential to success. He must know what, when, where, how, and whom he will teach. Some of the factors that should be considered are:
1) The objectives
2) The materials needed
3) The methods to be used
4) Employee participation
5) Employee interest
6) Training aids
7) Evaluation
8) Summarization

Employee preparation consists in preparing the employee to receive the material. Probably the most important single factor in the preparation of the employee is arousing and maintaining his interest. He must know the objectives of the training, why he is there, how the material can be used, and its importance to him.

b. Presentation
In presentation, have a carefully designed plan and follow it. The plan should be accurate and complete, yet flexible enough to meet situations as they arise. The method of presentation will be determined by the particular situation and objectives.

c. Summary
A summary should be made at the end of every training unit and program. In addition, there may be internal summaries depending on the nature of the material being taught. The important thing is that the trainee must always be able to understand how each part of the new material relates to the whole.

d. Application
The supervisor must arrange work so the employee will be given a chance to apply new knowledge or skills while the material is still clear in his mind and interest is high. The trainee does not really know whether he has learned the material until he has been given a chance to apply it. If the material is not applied, it loses most of its value.

e. Evaluation
The purpose of all training is to promote learning. To determine whether the training has been a success or failure, the supervisor must evaluate this learning.
In the broadest sense, evaluation includes all the devices, methods, skills, and techniques used by the supervisor to keep himself and the employees informed as to their progress toward the objectives they are pursuing. The extent to which the employee has mastered the knowledge, skills, and abilities, or changed his attitudes, as determined by the program objectives, is the extent to which instruction has succeeded or failed.
Evaluation should not be confined to the end of the lesson, day, or program but should be used continuously. We shall note later the way this relates to the rest of the teaching process.

2. Teaching Methods
A teaching method is a pattern of identifiable student and instructor activity used in presenting training material.
All supervisors are faced with the problem of deciding which method should be used at a given time.

a. Lecture
The lecture is direct oral presentation of material by the supervisor. The present trend is to place less emphasis on the trainer's activity and more on that of the trainee.

b. Discussion
Teaching by discussion or conference involves using questions and other techniques to arouse interest and focus attention upon certain areas, and by doing so creating a learning situation. This can be one of the most

valuable methods because it gives the employees an opportunity to express their ideas and pool their knowledge.

c. Demonstration
The demonstration is used to teach how something works or how to do something. It can be used to show a principle or what the results of a series of actions will be. A well-staged demonstration is particularly effective because it shows proper methods of performance in a realistic manner.

d. Performance
Performance is one of the most fundamental of all learning techniques or teaching methods. The trainee may be able to tell how a specific operation should be performed but he cannot be sure he knows how to perform the operation until he has done so.
As with all methods, there are certain advantages and disadvantages to each method.

e. Which Method to Use
Moreover, there are other methods and techniques of teaching. It is difficult to use any method without other methods entering into it. In any learning situation, a combination of methods is usually more effective than any one method alone.

Finally, evaluation must be integrated into the other aspects of the teaching-learning process.

It must be used in the motivation of the trainees; it must be used to assist in developing understanding during the training; and it must be related to employee application of the results of training.

This is distinctly the role of the supervisor.

www.ingramcontent.com/pod-product-compliance
Lightning Source LLC
Chambersburg PA
CBHW080321020526
44117CB00035B/2591